FREDERICK
CROWN PRINCE AND EMPEROR

FREDERICK
CROWN PRINCE
AND EMPEROR

A Biographical Sketch Dedicated to His Memory

BY

RENNELL RODD

WITH AN INTRODUCTION BY
HER MAJESTY
THE EMPRESS FREDERICK

AND A FOREWORD BY
JOHN VAN DER KISTE

'He was as full of kindness as of valour,
Princely in both.'

A & F Reprints

First published 1888 by David Stott
Revised edition published by A & F 2015

A & F Publications,
South Brent, Devon, England TQ10 9AS

Cover: *Crown Prince Frederick William at a Court Ball*, 1878,
by Anton von Werner

ISBN 9798648856295

Typeset 11pt Baskerville
Printed by CreateSpace

CONTENTS

Foreword to the 2015 edition   3
Introduction - Letter from Her Majesty the Empress
   Frederick   21
Preface   25

I.   1831-1848   27
II. 1848-1858   38
III. 1858-1863   53
IV. 1864-1869   65
V. 1870-1871   81
VI. 1871-1887   109
VII. 1888   129

Footnotes   138
Appendix: The Emperor Frederick's proclamation to
   his people   141
Rescript addressed to the Imperial Chancellor   144

FOREWORD

FREDERICK, Crown Prince and Emperor, by Rennell Rodd, was
the first biography of the second German Emperor to be
published, appearing five months after his untimely death in
June 1888. As the title suggested, it was no more than an
interim work, a tribute about 32,000 words in length. It was
written after the Empress Frederick and her brother Albert
Edward, Prince of Wales, had personally asked him to do so,
partly to honour his memory and partly to raise funds for the
Throat Hospital in London. The Empress may have been
partly the author of the work herself, and at least almost
certainly supplied some of the material. Bound in dark green
cloth, the front cover design was adorned with a small spray
of white heather which, as related in the second chapter, the
Prince had presented to her as he asked for her hand in
marriage thirty-three years earlier.

This new edition reproduces the full text of the original,
with very minor alterations such as the expansion of names
by adding forenames, and substituting 'King Ludwig II of
Bavaria' for 'the King of Bavaria', and modernisation of the
punctuation in some instances, like the substitution of single
inverted commas around quotations. Footnotes have been
moved from the foot of each page as applicable and placed
in a separate section at the end; as with names, some have
been slightly expanded from the originals, and I have added
a couple where I felt they would add clarity. The original

frontispiece with facsimile signature is reproduced herewith, while eight additional illustrations are included.

James Rennell Rodd was born in London on 9 November 1858, the only son of Major James Rennell Rodd (1812–1892) and his wife, the former Elizabeth Anne Thomson. He was educated at Haileybury and at Balliol College, Oxford, where he was awarded a third class in honour moderations in 1878 and a second class in *literae humaniores* in 1880. At first it seemed that his main vocation was likely to be as a poet. He won the Newdigate prize for English verse in 1880 with a poem on Sir Walter Raleigh, and while at college he was friends for a while with Oscar Wilde, who helped him in securing publication for his first book of verse, *Rose Leaf and Apple Leaf*, and contributed an introduction. Their association did not survive Wilde's fall from grace in 1895. At the same time he had several other contacts in the world of contemporary arts, including Edward Burne-Jones, who urged him to become a painter, and James Whistler.

Despite such creative leanings and the urging of others, he decided in favour of a career in diplomacy, and took the Foreign Office examination. He was failed the first time because his handwriting was so poor, but passed at his second attempt. In 1884 he took up his first post as a councillor at the embassy at Berlin, where he became a close friend of the then German Crown Prince and Princess Frederick William, as he later came to describe in his memoirs:

A few days after my arrival the military Attaché, Colonel, afterwards General, Sir Leopold Swaine, took me to the Neues Palais at Wildpark, near Potsdam, the summer residence of the Crown Prince Frederick. The Crown Princess invited members of our Embassy to play tennis there and remain to supper once or twice every week. This was my introduction to a long series of similar pleasant parties, at which all ceremony was dispensed with. Vivid still remains the impression made upon me by the Crown Prince when for the first time I saw him approaching the tennis ground with his four Italian greyhounds, a splendid figure of dignified manhood, radiating kindliness with a friendly smile. One had only to see him to understand that his influence had been exerted, so far as his authority extended with his own army, on the side of humanity and in the defence of historic monuments during the war of '70. At supper, an unconventional meal, which began with curded milk and tea and went on to hot dishes and wine, I sat next to the Crown Princess and fell at once under the charm of one of the most cultivated women I have ever met, whose intelligent eyes had an irresistible appeal in them. The three unmarried daughters were present, and the simple natural intercourse of that happy family circle disarmed any shyness incidental to a first meeting. Free of address and inviting unrestricted discussion, the Crown Princess had nevertheless that unconscious habit of Royalty, the prerogative of always being right, as I was to learn without delay.[1]

With regard to relationships and personalities within the imperial family, Rodd proved to be an astute judge of character. On his regular visits to the family at the Neues Palais, Potsdam, on the edge of Berlin, he soon saw for himself that the Crown Princess and her eldest son Prince William were 'in certain respects temperamentally too much alike ever to get on. She was an idealist, lacking in worldly wisdom, and therefore often indiscreet. [William] was also an idealist, but his idealism was vitiated by a self-assurance which did not allow him to question the rightness of his own conclusions. Both were impetuous and impatient of opposition.'[2]

During his years in Berlin he gave them both considerable moral support, especially once the Crown Prince became ill in 1887 and died on 15 June 1888, three months after succeeding his ninety-year-old father William as Emperor. When Queen Victoria announced her intention of coming to visit her daughter and dying son-in-law in Berlin in April 1888, Bismarck and his colleagues were angry, and there was speculation that she might be prevented from coming, or that Bismarck would cause a governmental crisis by resigning, or to threatening to do so if she did set foot in Berlin. If this had happened, the Empress, already known by her detractors as *die Engländerin*, would be vilified even more by those who were accusing her of trying to subvert the German court to undue English influence. 'People professed to love and to admire the Emperor Frederick,' Rodd noted, 'and yet they could not resist embittering his last days by abusing the Empress.'[3] Queen Victoria refused to be put off, she paid her visit as scheduled, and she not only saw Emperor Frederick for what they knew would be the last time, but also had a perfectly amicable audience with Bismarck, who had initially been quite nervous at the prospect of meeting her. Rodd wrote afterwards that he had never seen the people of Berlin so enthusiastic as they were when Queen and Empress appeared in public together, 'and their cheers were a striking answer to the pessimists who had asserted that the Empress dared not show herself and that the Queen would do well not to come.'[4]

He visited the widowed Empress at Friedrichskron shortly after the Emperor's funeral, and it was on this occasion that she suggested the idea of this book. As he recalled, she told him

[...] she was anxious to do something for the benefit of the Hospital for Diseases of the Throat, and asked me to write a biography of the Emperor Frederick, for which she would herself prepare an introduction. The proceeds of the sale would be given to the funds of the Hospital. The Prince of Wales before leaving Berlin had also mentioned this matter to me and expressed the wish

6

that I should undertake it. I could not of course do so without the authorization of the Secretary of State for Foreign Affairs. But Lord Salisbury readily assented to the proposal.[5]

Frederick, Crown Prince and Emperor was published on 16 November that year, much to the displeasure of the young Emperor William II. He had seen his father's reign as a short but unwelcome hiatus in the history of his kingdom and empire, and unlike his widowed mother he was not anxious for Emperor Frederick to be remembered, let alone celebrated. Nevertheless, translations in German and French were published simultaneously. As a subsequent biographer of the Empress observed, it was characteristic of the official prevailing attitude in Germany in those days that the first biography of her second Emperor had to be written by an Englishman.[6] The second, more lengthy life, *'Fritz' of Prussia: Germany's Second Emperor*, by Lucy Taylor, was published three years later. It was followed by a three-volume life by Margaretha von Poschinger towards the end of the decade, and a one-volume edition by Sidney Whitman, *Life of the Emperor Frederick*, appeared in 1901.

Three subsequent lives in English have appeared since then, *Frederick III; German Emperor 1888* (1981), by the present author, *Frederick III: Germany's Liberal Emperor* (1995), by Patricia Kollander, and *Our Fritz*, by Frank Muller (2011). Two volumes of translations of his writings have been published, namely extracts from his diaries for the campaigns of 1866 and 1870-1 and his journeys to the east and to Spain, in 1902, and a fuller one for his 1870-1 war diary, in 1927. It is perhaps significant that the Empress Frederick has attracted several more biographers, among them an anonymous chronicler (1913), E.E.P. Tisdall (1940), Richard Barkeley (1956), Conte Egon Caesar Corti (1957), Daphne Bennett (1971), Andrew Sinclair (1981), and Hannah Pakula (1996), and her correspondence with Queen Victoria and with her second daughter Sophie,

7

Queen of Greece runs to several volumes. There has also been one joint life of the couple, the present author's *Dearest Vicky, Darling Fritz* (2001).

On its appearance in Britain, *The Times* called Rodd's book a 'small memorial volume', and 'essentially a simple, straightforward record [...] It is the very reverse of polemical or controversial; as may be gauged from the fact that neither Prince Bismarck nor Sir Morell Mackenzie is once mentioned in it.'[7] It did include the Emperor's rescript to Bismarck as an appendix, and as the reviewer failed to notice, he was referred to albeit in passing in the narrative. Otto von Bismarck, the imperial Chancellor, had been politically at odds with Frederick as Crown Prince ever since his appointment to office in 1862. Mackenzie, the British doctor summoned to attend Frederick during his illness, had fallen out with the German doctors, and published a stout defence of his management of the case, *The Fatal Illness of Frederick the Noble*, a month earlier. By doing so he had alienated much of his professional support at the time when he needed it most, irritated Queen Victoria and privately distressed the Empress Frederick. It was therefore important that Rodd's perfectly anodyne account sought to avoid any controversy.

At the end of Chapter III, he noted that 'Of the relation of the Crown Prince to political life it does not enter into the design of the present sketch to speak'. His reference to Bismarck being appointed head of government in 1862 made no allusion to King William's threat to abdicate if he did not get his way over the Prussian constitutional crisis, and let his astonished, quite unprepared son and heir become King. Likewise, any allusion to the 'Danzig incident', the Crown Prince's denunciation of Bismarck's decree curtailing the freedom of the press in Prussia a year later, is omitted, and his account of the Emperor's funeral, which he called 'solemn and impressive', was restraint itself. He would leave it to later biographers to describe the undignified ceremony, held with undue haste three days later, for which no invitations had been sent out to other European sovereigns or princes. The Prince and Princess of Wales and their eldest son Prince Albert Victor, who had known the end was near, were among the few royalties from outside Germany present. Bismarck did not bother to attend, sending his son Herbert, German Secretary of State for Foreign Affairs, to represent him. Before the obsequies began, the younger Bismarck was noticed talking and laughing with the clergymen as they waited for the coffin to arrive. In order to discourage spectators, Emperor William II had had the route of the funeral procession cordoned off by soldiers. The widowed Empress and her unmarried daughters could not bear to attend, and instead held a private service of their own at Bornstedt.

As a biography, Rodd's volume is indeed the opposite of controversial, and therefore far from complete. Nevertheless, as a touching tribute and short record of other aspects of his life, notably his role in the wars fought by Prussia between 1864 and 1871, it fulfils its purpose.

Rodd had met Mackenzie briefly on one occasion in Berlin, shortly after the Emperor Frederick's accession to the throne in March. Having done so, he was able to form his opinion of the doctor which concurred with that of so many others, and felt he was

[...] a strong and masterful personality, but not to me a sympathetic one. Due allowance must be made for the difficulty of his position. While he retained the entire confidence of the Emperor and Empress to the last and he had certainly preserved his patient's life long enough to secure his succession there was hardly anyone in Berlin who took his side. I could not but resent the manner in which he repeatedly pressed his claims for a decoration, as though he seemed to be anxious lest the end should come before he received it. Chauvinism and racial feeling no doubt played an undue part in the medical controversy. But he did not improve his position

9

by his own want of tact in many details.[8]

He was similarly unimpressed by Mackenzie's book

[…] dealing with his experience of the case, which served no good purpose, and which was severely judged as a breach of medical etiquette by the faculty in England. A British medical friend of very clear and impartial judgment, who studied the documents at the time, told me that he considered, apart from the question of whether the premises postulated were correct, the report of the German doctors to be a model of what such a medical statement should be, clear and complete, whereas the hysterical exposition of Mackenzie condemned itself.[9]

Two months after Rodd's publication, it was brought to his notice that a letter he had quoted from at length (see below, p.105) was open to question. It had been supposedly written by the late Madame André Walther, referring to Crown Prince Frederick at Versailles during the Franco-Prussian war, regularly quoted in the press during the previous eighteen years and assumed to be authentic. A few weeks after the publication of his book, Rodd received a letter from her son, in which he declared that the letter was 'entirely apocryphal as far as Madame André Walther is concerned, inasmuch that the lady was never at Versailles throughout the siege of Paris, and he considers that it implies a reflection on the memory and patriotism of this much respected lady, which the family cannot allow to pass unnoticed.' He regretted the insertion of the letter, and at having unconsciously wounded the feelings of the family, in a book in which he 'had endeavoured to avoid all controversial matter'.[10]

By this time, Rodd's service in Germany was almost over.

My four years at the Embassy now drew to an end, and I was not altogether sorry to leave. Under actual conditions the atmosphere of Berlin was far from sympathetic to me and, interesting as the moment of transition might be, I was better pleased to watch it from without. Unwittingly I found myself rapidly becoming a courtier, whereas nature had meant me for a Bohemian.[11]

He had just been promoted to the post of second secretary at Athens. Three years later he went to Rome, which he had visited twice, some nine and ten years earlier. In 1892 he transferred to Paris, but was only there briefly as in 1893 he was given charge of the British agency at Zanzibar and appointed acting commissioner for British East Africa. During his time there he was in command of the expedition that summer known as the second Witu campaign, the result of a territorial dispute, and was present at two skirmishes at Pumwani and Jongeni.

In 1894 he was transferred to Cairo, where he worked under Lord Cromer, Consul-General of Egypt, and took charge during his absences on leave. His first important mission came three years later, when he was sent to Abyssinia as a special envoy with responsibility for negotiating a treaty with Emperor Menelik II. He secured permanent British representation at the Emperor's court, a most-favoured-nation arrangement in regard to commerce, the prevention of war munitions for the Mahdists passing through Abyssinia, and a delineation of frontiers on the north and east of that country. For his efforts he was rewarded by his appointment as Companion of the Order of the Bath (CB) and in 1899 as Knight Commander of the Order of St Michael and St George (KCMG) for his management of the work in the agency at Cairo during the Fashoda crisis.

After having worked in Africa for several years, he

returned to Rome in 1902 as first secretary. In this capacity he was responsible for the successful negotiation several treaties of delimitation of African territories with the Italian government. Promoted to the rank of Counsellor, he was appointed Plenipotentiary to Sweden and Norway in 1904, and he arrived in Stockholm to take up his post in January 1905.

It was to be a demanding time, for his main task during the next few months was to play an active and neutral part in the dissolution of the union between both Scandinavian countries which took effect at the end of the year. Accomplishing a difficult task with tact and diplomacy, he was rewarded with the Grand Cross of the Victorian Order in England by King Edward VII and the Grand Cross of the Order of the Polar Star by King Oscar II in Sweden. He remained as Minister at Stockholm until 1908, when on his return to England he was sworn of the Privy Council. Appointed Ambassador to Italy, he stayed there throughout the years of World War One and remained until 1919. It proved to be the most notable appointment in his career, as during his tenure of the embassy at Rome, not only did he prove to be popular and well-liked by all, but his judgment was invaluable to the British government in the months leading up to Italy joining the allies in 1915.

Shortly after this he began writing his memoirs. In these he gave a modest account of his role in persuading key Italian ministers that it would be in Italy's interests to join the allies in spite of pressure exerted by Germans. They had sent Bernhard von Bülow, a former German foreign minister and imperial chancellor, to Rome as ambassador with the special mission of preventing what they saw as an Italian defection. When he failed to do so, Rodd was the subject of fierce cartoons in the German press, depicting him as a tyrant and bully. He had however refrained from exerting direct pressure on the Italian government, as he was convinced that true national interests would cause them to choose the allied side in spite of their economic weakness and lack of adequate military preparation.

At the end of his service in Italy, he could look back not only on this diplomatic success but also on the earlier establishment in Rome of two institutions which subsequently proved of no little value to the cultural relations between Italy and the United Kingdom. One was the Keats–Shelley Association, established in 1908, based at Keats's house by the Spanish Steps. The other was the British School of Archaeology and the Arts, created in 1911. As a published poet and a spare-time archaeologist, both of these owed much to his well-informed support and passion. When he left the embassy in 1919, he was transferred to Viscount Milner's special commission on the status of Egypt. Having been promoted Knight Grand Cross of the Order of the Bath (GCB) in the new year's honours list in 1920, he retired from the diplomatic service in 1921.

His skills ensured that retirement did not mean the end of his career, and his talents would still be used in foreign affairs. In 1921 and 1923 he was a representative of the British government at the general assembly of the League of Nations; in 1925 he was president of the court of conciliation between Austria and Switzerland; in 1928 he sat on the permanent commission of conciliation between Italy and Chile; and he was a member of the permanent international commission for the advancement of peace between the United States and Venezuela.

During these years he was briefly implicated, albeit innocently, of what was called 'one of the most impudent literary forgeries on record'.[12] In 1926 Hesketh Pearson, at that time a struggling actor and biographer of radical views and little respect for authority, delivered the manuscript of his newest work, *The Whispering Gallery: Leaves from a Diplomat's Diary*, to his publishers, the Bodley Head. It purported to be the anything but flattering recollections of friends, acquaintances in social and diplomatic circles, crowned heads and senior statesmen, and others throughout Europe. He stipulated that it must be published

13

anonymously, but told them in confidence that it was the work of Sir Rennell Rodd. Recognising a bestseller when they saw it, the Bodley Head were happy to publish, but some of the more scurrilous assertions, or as one reviewer saw fit to pronounce, 'a libel on almost every page', forced them to think again. Another denounced the author 'an imposter and a cad', and called the book 'an unscrupulous farrago'. It would not have escaped the notice of many potential readers that Rodd, having already published his never less than respectful memoirs in three volumes, was hardly likely to follow them up with a single volume of gossip which had surely been calculated to provoke if not give offence in certain quarters, an action which would jeopardise his position as an honourable figure in public life.

A representative of the publishers had no alternative but to break the author's confidence and pay Rodd a personal visit at his home, informing him that he had been identified as the real writer. An angry Rodd exonerated himself by publishing a letter in *The Times* in which he expressed his surprise that in view of his long record of public service the publishers 'could for a moment have entertained the idea that I could be responsible for a volume of this deplorable character'.[13] He also denied he had even met Pearson, although he could not be certain as in a busy life and career he had met many well-known people in passing. Lord Northcliffe, owner of the *Daily Mail*, had taken exception to some of the allegations Pearson had made about him, and threatened to sue for libel. The book was therefore withdrawn and in 1927 Pearson, having repaid the publisher his £250 advance before a criminal charge could be brought against him, was put on trial for attempted fraud. He pleaded not guilty on the grounds that he must have been mad – his family had recommended that he should use insanity as a mitigating circumstance, brought on by the head wounds he had suffered while fighting in the war - and was acquitted.

As far as Rodd was concerned, that was the end of the

matter, although in a subsequent letter he deprecated the inconvenience and annoyance caused to him by being falsely credited as the author of the book. He had been detained in England and forced to change plans at short notice, had unnecessarily spent much valuable time in the law courts, had been given 'a publicity of a kind which I am old-fashioned enough to dislike', and further time had been wasted in telephone calls and demands for interviews on the matter, yet had no means of obtaining any redress. He was also irritated that one of his sons had also been named as the author, and that the rumour had gained currency.[14] Pearson had inevitably damaged his career as a writer in the short term, and for a few years no publisher would consider a new title from him, but after a few years of being in disgrace he found renewed success as a biographer. In his earlier days he had believed that the biographer and historian were justified in using invention whenever it could 'improve on fact', but later he revised his views. Although he died in 1964, some of his books are still widely read and, like *The Whispering Gallery* (with a title page, if not the cover, no longer hiding behind the mask of anonymity) have recently been brought back into print by other publishers.

In his seventieth year yet another career for Rodd beckoned, this time at Westminster. Turning to domestic politics, he stood for Parliament and represented Marylebone as a Conservative from 1928 to 1932, winning a by-election on 30 April 1928 in a three-cornered contest and securing a majority of 6,138, which he increased handsomely in a general election the following year to 15,287. He stood down in 1932, and a year later he was raised to the peerage as Baron Rennell of Rodd, in the county of Hereford.

Throughout these years and the occasionally recurrent controversies about the Emperor Frederick and his family, usually following the publication of relevant biographies, he continued to spring eloquently to their defence in *The Times*. When Emil Ludwig's *Kaiser Wilhelm II* was published in

15

1926, Rodd reviewed the book and questioned the accuracy of several statements. He stated that Crown Princess Frederick William had come to luncheon at the British Embassy early in 1887 to attend a christening and how, when they spoke about the Crown Prince's illness, the Chief Ambassador, Sir Edward Malet, suggested the possibility of obtaining another opinion and the Crown Princess said she did not know who the best authorities would be. Shortly after the luncheon, Bismarck paid a visit to Malet and informed him that arrangements had just been made for a British specialist, the noted laryngologist Dr Morell Mackenzie, to come to Berlin and examine him. At that time Mackenzie was regarded as the foremost European practitioner in his field. In view of assertions thereafter that the Crown Princess had deliberately sent for Mackenzie because she did not trust German doctors or specialists, Rodd's statement was important in establishing beyond doubt that she had previously been unaware of his existence, and that the summons to him was entirely due to German initiatives.[15] As he observed, one word from the German Chancellor at the time would have clarified the matter beyond all doubt, but 'Bismarck, we know, never allowed sentiment to intervene when political ends were to be gained'.[16]

In January 1932 the Emperor Frederick's third daughter Sophie, the exiled former Queen of Greece, died in Florence. During the First World War she had been accused by the Allied Powers of exerting undue influence on her husband, King Constantine, and trying to persuade him to commit Greece to joining the conflict on the side of Germany, and after they were deposed and went into exile they were shunned by the British community overseas as a result. Within a week of her death, Rodd exonerated her from this charge, observing in a lengthy letter that

Circumstances allowed her no opportunity of refuting opinions or disavowing actions attributed to her, and the last ten years of a broken life were passed in quiet dignity and commendable reserve as an exile in a hospitable foreign country, under circumstances pathetically different from those she had seemed entitled to anticipate.[17]

Apart from his diplomatic services Rodd was also a published poet and prolific author. Between 1881 and 1940 he published some twenty volumes, including several collections of poems, of which those to become the best-known were *Feda* (1886), *The Unknown Madonna* (1888), *Ballads of the Fleet* (1897), *Myrtle and Oak* (1902), the introduction to an anthology of verse by English poets, *An Englishman in* Greece (1910), and some renderings from the Greek anthology, *Love, Worship and Death* (1916). His classical and medieval studies bore fruit in *Customs and Lore of Modern Greece* (1892) and *The Princes of Achaia and the Chronicles of Morea* (2 vols., 1907). His detailed knowledge of the city of Rome was exhibited in what outside learned circles is probably his best-known work, *Rome of the Renaissance and of Today* (1932). In later years he himself took most pride in his scholarly *Homer's Ithaca: A Vindication of Tradition* (1927), and he was also the author of a biography of *Sir Walter Raleigh* (1921). His reminiscences, *Social and Diplomatic Memories*, published in three volumes between 1922 and 1925, gave a full account of the years of his official life. In his spare time he also enjoyed archaeology and sailing yachts.

Rodd had married Lilias Georgina Guthrie, daughter of James Alexander Guthrie, in 1894, and they had a family of four sons and two daughters. His third son, Peter, was married to the author Nancy Mitford for a while, though it ended in divorce. His elder daughter, Evelyn Emmet, followed him to Westminster as a Conservative MP for East Grinstead, and after resigning her seat she was created a life peer, Baroness Emmet of Amberley.

Rodd died at Ardath, Shamley Green, Surrey, on 26 July 1941, aged 82, and was succeeded in the barony by his second son Francis, a future President of the Royal Geographical Society. His death marked the end of an era in that he was the last of the surviving ambassadors at the courts of Europe on the outbreak of war in 1914. Tributes were paid to a diplomat and scholar of great distinction, and a 'courteous, unassuming, modest, but resolute' man who 'quickly won the devotion of his subordinates, the respect of the statesmen with whom he had to deal, and the affection of the learned men at Rome.'[18]

REFERENCES

1. Rodd, Rennell, *Social and Diplomatic Memories, 1884-1893* (London, Edward Arnold, 1922, 48-9)
2. ibid, 50
3. ibid, 133
4. ibid, 149
5. ibid, 149-50
6. Barkeley, Richard, *The Empress Frederick* (London, Macmillan, 1956, 265)
7. *The Times*, 16.11.1988
8. Rodd, 131
9. ibid, 151
10. *The Times*, 2.2.1889
11. Rodd, 163
12. Pearson, Hesketh, *The Whispering Gallery* (London, Phoenix, 2000, xxi)
13. *The Times*, 23.11.1926
14. ibid, 29.1.1927
15. *The Times*, 1.12.1926; *Letters of the Empress Frederick*, edited by Sir Frederick Ponsonby (London, Macmillan, 1928, 228-30)
16. *The Times*, 25.11.1926

17. ibid, 18.1.1932
18. *Oxford Dictionary of National Biography*

John Van der Kiste
2015

SCHLOSS FRIEDRICHSKRON,

August 18th, 1888.

Dear Mr. Rodd,

I think you are aware that my beloved husband, the late Emperor Frederick, when in England last year, visited the Throat Hospital, and was full of compassion for the patients. His ailment caused at that time but little inconvenience, and his kind heart felt deeply sorry for those who had more to bear from the state of their throats. I had then a great wish to help the Hospital in some way, and had intended to make some little drawings, and collect some pretty and amusing stories to form a small book which could be sold for the benefit of the Hospital funds. Alas! I never found leisure or peace of mind to carry out this plan.

As I have witnessed how much can be done by medical skill and careful nursing to alleviate the condition of those who suffer, I feel doubly anxious that as many as possible of those who have to struggle with sickness should he able to gain admission to a Hospital where they can find care and comforts which they could not have at home, and the best chance of being cured. Now that I have seen the kind and sincere sympathy with which my own countrymen followed the course of my beloved husband's illness, and the true feeling they showed in mourning his loss, I feel emboldened to take up under another form my idea of helping the Hospital. Not my own drawings or writings would I offer, but I ask you to pen a short account of the life of my beloved husband, who was so soon taken away from us. As you knew him in sunny days when he was the picture of life and health, as well as in the last sad year when that life was overshadowed by sickness, I thought none would be better able than you to undertake the task of writing a short biography suitable for popular reading, which may make his name better known to the English Public, and give him a place in their affections beside that of my father, for whom he had so great a love, admiration and veneration, and with whose views and aims he so truly sympathized. I feel sure that the life of a good and noble man must he interesting to all, and that an example so bright and pure can only do good.

Those in humbler walks of life who are denied many of the blessings enjoyed by the rich, to whose lot fall the so-called good things of this world, are often apt to imagine that their burden is the hardest to bear, that struggles, and pain, and tears are only for them. These perhaps will think differently when they read of sufferings borne with such patience, and of duty so cheerfully performed while sickness was undermining the strength of the strong man; they will be able to enter in some degree into the depths of regret and disappointment felt by a ruler who loved his people, at being unable to carry out the long- cherished plans for the welfare that he had so much at heart; they will gaze with admiration at the courage with which, when the shades of death were hanging over his path, he strode stedfastly along to the end.

Grief and pain come alike to all; broken hearts are to

22

be found in palaces as well as in cottages, and the bond of brotherhood seems strongest when love and pity unite all hearts, and reverence for what is good lifts up our souls. May this little history of the good and useful life of the Emperor Frederick appeal to the hearts of those who read it, and be as it were a greeting from him to his fellow sufferers in the Hospital, to whom I so earnestly desire to do a small service; and to which you have so kindly promised to devote your pen.

Yours sincerely,

Victoria

PREFACE

The following brief sketch contains nothing controversial, nothing which could lead to dispute or discussion, and it has been especially attempted to eliminate, as far as possible, all matter of a political nature, and confine it to the record of such facts as illustrate the character of a simple and noble life, in a manner which may be acceptable to that wider circle of readers for whom, in accordance with the desire expressed in the introduction, it is designed. It is incomplete, inasmuch as it contains the story of one life, which is so intimately bound up with another, that the picture could only be completed by a full account of the lives of both. But it is believed that the intention of one, in obedience to whose wishes it was undertaken, has been thus best fulfilled.

R. R.

October, 1888.

I.

1831—1848.

THE Emperor Frederick was born on the 18th of October, 1831, the anniversary of the battle of Leipzig, and on the 18th of June, 1888, the anniversary of the battle of Waterloo, he was carried to his last resting-place in the church dedicated to Peace, among the gardens of Sans Souci. It is a curious coincidence that a life which will be for ever associated in history with the union of the German race into the great Empire of today should have opened and closed upon the anniversaries of these two great victories. In the fierce light of modern days, when nothing remains secret or sacred, where every action is watched by a thousand jealous eyes, interpreted or misinterpreted by a thousand busy voices, we do not always recognize our heroes when they come: but the immediate verdict of contemporaries found him worthy of the time he was born in, and of the great events he was called upon to assist in moulding. Placed in that lofty station which at least escapes the eye of scrutiny, he was found true to his own princely ideal as son, as husband, as father; true to the ideal of his countrymen as a fearless leader in the battlefield, true to the highest ideal of all times as man and prince; and surely, wherever the story is told of the great decade which closed with the proclamation of the German Empire at Versailles, beside the three figures which dominate it, the darling hero of future generations of Germans will be the Prince who taught the North and South their common brotherhood, whom Saxons, Bavarians, Württembergers, and Badenese, no less than Prussians, alike saluted by the name of 'Unser Fritz.'

Those who have witnessed the events of the last months, have all been touched according to the depth of their own natures by the brave endurance and resignation, by the deeply pathetic close of a life, which, with its great opportunities for good and evil, was spent in unceasing devotion to duty, in patient preparation for yet greater responsibilities, in unwearying efforts for the good of others. And yet probably what will remain to after generations, when the passions and emotions of life around them engage all their attention, and the keen interest with which we have followed the events of the past year is absorbed in other lives, will be that radiant and heroic figure, which children's eyes will follow on the canvases depicting the triumph of Germany, of the soldier-prince, who, in the hour of danger and uncertainty, succeeded in uniting the sympathies of North and South, and guided that irresistible wave of national feeling through the bloody fields of Weissenburg and Wörth, by the great strategic march to the crowning victory of Sedan, It may not be the immortality he would himself have chosen, but no man is master of his fate, and where so much must needs be left undone, where so many hopes and aspirations were disappointed, this at least will remain for ever associated with the most imperishable traditions of a great nation, of a Prince who did all things well. History has but few such figures to show us, and the record of their lives is soon told. The evil genius of many of the great characters of story has filled innumerable volumes, but a few lines will keep green the memory of our Sydneys and our Bayards. As with nations, we say they are happiest who afford least material to the historian; so perhaps with great men, in proportion to the nobility and simplicity of their lives the work of the biographer becomes easier, and truly of the Emperor Frederick, we may say as of few others who have lived so much before the world:

> 'He kept
> 'The whiteness of his soul, and thus men o'er
>   him wept.'

In the year that ushered in the birth of the young Prince, the most sanguine of patriots would scarcely have ventured to prophecy the imminent ascendency of the Prussian star. King Frederick William III, who had already occupied the throne for thirty-four years, had seen the disastrous days of Jena and Auerstadt, and had devoted himself to the great task of the restoration of his country. He had shared in the victories which ended in the overthrow of Napoleon, and after the long and troublous reign, which he epitomized himself in one proverbial sentence, 'My days in unrest, but my hope in God,' desired only to end his life in peace.

The dream of German unity had made but little progress. It was the interest of Austria and Russia to see that their Prussian neighbour should find no means of expansion, and the conservatism of the smaller German states looked with no friendly eye on a capital where the spirit of opposition to the old order was most rife, and the speeches and writings of the new school of politicians assumed a more violent character.

The Crown Prince had married some eight years previously Princess Elizabeth of Bavaria, and the marriage had remained childless. His younger brother Prince William was therefore the heir presumptive, and it was the occasion for no ordinary rejoicing when his marriage with Princess Augusta of Saxe-Weimar was blessed two years later with the birth of a son, and a direct hereditary succession was thus guaranteed in the house of Hohenzollern.

The Prince was born in the palace to which as Emperor he gave the name of Friedrichskron, known till then only as the New Palace of Sans Souci, the largest and the finest of the many palaces of Potsdam, to which his parents had then retired on account of the cholera, which was raging at that time in Berlin. It was built by Frederick the Great immediately after the close of the Seven Years' War, to the confusion of those who thought that his treasury was exhausted, but which had hitherto been little used. It was this palace that in later years, as Crown Prince, the Emperor Frederick made his summer residence; here most of his children were born, here all the interests and pursuits of country life were fostered and enjoyed, here were the brightest associations of a happy home, and it was hither that he came to die. The Mark of Brandenburg is for the most part a flat unlovely district of sanely plains alternating with wide tracts of fir forest, but, in the neighbourhood of Potsdam, the river Havel, widening in a series of considerable lakes surrounded with undulating wooded shores, has formed a pleasant oasis, and there are few prettier spots in the early summer months than the gardens and Park of Sans Souci, at the further end of which, about a mile and a half from Potsdam, stands the great Rococo Palace of Friedrichskron.

The christening took place on the 13th of November, in the presence of the King, the Crown Prince, and all the members of the Royal Family. The absent godparents, the Empresses of Austria and Russia, were represented by their respective Ambassadors, and the baby Prince received from Bishop Eylert the names of Frederick William Nicholas Charles.

The Princes of the House of Hohenzollern become soldiers almost from the cradle. Prince William, who had, while still a mere boy, entered Paris with the Allies, took a keen delight in the military education of his son, and the little Prince was only eight years old when, together with two young playfellows,[1] he was put through his drill in a miniature private's uniform, and acquitted himself as a most capable recruit, under the orders of his instructor. Sergeant Bludau. Of the qualities which he inherited from his parents it is not necessary to speak. The courage, simplicity, integrity, and kindliness of the aged Emperor, who was in a truer sense than any who have borne the title the 'father of his people,' are known to all the present generation. But of the friends and playfellows of his youth many have now passed away, and it may be interesting here to record that there was no one to whom, in these early days, he was more fondly attached than Princess Charlotte of Prussia, who afterwards became Hereditary Princess of Meiningen, and mother of his future son-in-law. He was also much with his cousins Prince Frederick Charles and the two sisters of the latter. Princess, afterwards Queen Elizabeth, the wife of King Frederick William IV, had no children of her own, but it was her especial pleasure to gather her young nephews and nieces round her, and be a second mother to them.

Prince Frederick William never forgot her kindness to him as a child; and when she died at Dresden, in 1873, after twelve years of widowhood, he took upon himself the duties of a son, and performed the last offices of kindness, bringing home her body to lay it beside her husband in the Church of Peace, at Sans Souci. The friendship formed in childhood for his cousin, Prince Frederick Charles, continued into later life, when their mimic games of war, with their respective corps of cadets, became the grim earnest of the battlefield. They were appointed Field-Marshals upon the same day, when the news of the fall of Metz reached the headquarters of the German Army at Versailles; and by a singular coincidence their deaths took place on the same day of the month, and at the same hour of the day, at the same interval of three years that had separated their births.

The education of Prince Frederick William began under the auspices of Frau von Clausewitz, widow of the well-known General, and Madame Godet, his governess, a Swiss lady from Neufchatel, whose son became, a few years later, the Prince's first tutor. In 1844, when he had reached his thirteenth year, the noted German Hellenist, Dr. Ernest Curtius, was chosen to superintend his studies. No branch of general culture was neglected; music and dancing, gymnastics and fencing, were all taught betimes, and the handicraft of bookbinding was selected for the young Prince to master, in accordance with the family tradition that all the Princes of the Royal House shall acquire practical knowledge of some trade.

In the meantime several events occurred to break

the quiet routine of study. In 1838 a sister was born, and christened Louise, after her grandmother, the Queen, whose beauty, courage and misfortunes, have made her the heroine of Prussian patriotism. In 1840 King Frederick William III died, and the little Prince was, for the first time, brought face to face with death. In accordance with precedent, Prince William now assumed the title of Prince of Prussia, and he was appointed by his brother, who had ascended the throne under the name of Frederick William IV, Stadtholder of Pomerania. On reaching his tenth year, Prince Frederick William received a commission as Second Lieutenant in the First Regiment of the Infantry of the Guard. He was presented to the officers of the regiment by his uncle, the King, who said to him: 'You are but a little fellow as yet, Fritz, but do your best to get to know these gentlemen, and some day you will be their overseer, however much they may now see over you.'

A military instructor was now attached to the Prince in the person of Colonel, afterwards General von Unruh, in company with whom, or with his tutor, Dr. Curtius, he began to make short journeys in the neighbouring provinces and states. Thus he visited the towns and islands of the Baltic, and made walking tours through the Harz, Thuringia, Saxon Switzerland, and the Giant Mountains, acquiring that taste for travel which he preserved in later years, and studying by personal observation 'the cities and customs of many men.' Otherwise, his summers were spent at Babelsberg, in the neighbourhood of Potsdam, the country seat which the Prince of Prussia had himself planned and executed, and which became his favourite country residence as King and Emperor.

It was here that the young Prince remained in seclusion with his mother through the troubled days of 1848, when the February Revolution at Paris gave the signal for outbreaks in other continental cities. The concessions which the Liberal Party had anticipated from the reigning Sovereign had not been granted, and the insurrectionists were for a time masters of the situation in Berlin. A spirit of self-sacrifice induced the Prince of Prussia to take upon himself a large portion of the popular resentment, and the future hero of German unity lightened his brother's task in re-establishing order, by withdrawing for a while from Berlin, and appearing to remove in his person the menace of the military element, against which a great part of the general discontent was directed. His intrepid character, however, resented giving colour to the appearance of flight, and he only left on receiving written orders from the King to proceed immediately upon a special mission to London, and report to the Court of St. James on recent developments at Berlin.

Prince Frederick William was then just at that age when, on the threshold of manhood, the mind is most impressionable, and, unbiased by the teachings of past experience, is apt to review with an immediate judgment the merits of current events. The scenes which he had lately witnessed could not fail to have a deep and lasting effect upon his generous and reflective character. The Throne recovered its ascendancy, but only after large concessions and a reform of the Constitution; the national voice had found expression, and a new phase of national development opened for the new generation. Early in June the Prince of Prussia returned, and signified his adhesion to the remodelled Constitution; the Princess, with her children, travelled as far as Magdeburg to

34

greet him on his return, and the rest of the summer was spent at Babelsberg, where the young Prince was prepared for his Confirmation, which took place in the chapel at Charlottenburg on September 29th. In the Spring of the following year, he was present at the solemn audience at which King Frederick William IV refused the Imperial Crown of Germany, which the Frankfort Parliament proposed to confer upon him, little anticipating how fully, some twenty years later, the words which fell from his uncle's lips were destined to be realized: *'An Imperial Crown must be won upon the field of battle.'*

The Prince was now in his eighteenth year, the age at which the Royal Princes enter upon active service in the army. His military education had been completed under General von Unruh, and, afterwards, under Major von Natzmer and Colonel Fischer - and so the chapter of boyhood closes. It cannot close better than with a quotation from a letter which the Princess of Prussia wrote to the playfellow and comrade of her son, Rudolf von Zastrow, who was also entering the world, and about to pass his examinations for the army, for it illustrates the nature of the home-influences under which their youth had passed.

'Life is full of difficulties and seductions of every kind, we must therefore daily pray for strength to combat them, that we may remain true to our principles. The superficialities of life often neutralize our taste for serious occupation; we must remember that we have something to learn every day, and that we shall not retain what we have learnt, if we fail to make our knowledge complete. What is most of all to be desired is the harmonious union of character and heart. Happy are they to whom God grants these qualities. I believe that you possess them. My prayer is that you may always be a son to me, and that separation may not weaken this tie. In me you will always find a friend, a mother. And next I pray you always to remain a friend, a brother, to my son. Princes seldom have real friends, his heart requires a friendship of this kind, and you may serve him in a number of ways. You have promised me this, and I rely upon your gratitude as well as your word of honour.'[2]

Prince Frederick William of Prussia, c.1840

II.

1848 —1858.

O N the 3rd of May, 1849, Prince Frederick William entered upon active service with the regiment to which he was attached. The Prince of Prussia introduced him to the assembled officers with a few spirited words, in which he spoke feelingly of the admirable discipline shown by the army in the recent troubles, and of the sympathy and fidelity which his old comrades had testified towards himself. 'I entrust my son to you,' he said, "in the hope that he will learn obedience, and so some day know how to command;' and to his son he simply said, 'Now go and do your duty!' A month later the Prince was advanced to the rank of First Lieutenant. The Prince of Prussia was at this period appointed to command the army sent to put down the military insurrection in Baden. He was accompanied on this expedition by the young Prince Frederick Charles, who was three years senior to his cousin. Twenty years later the two Princes received the Field-Marshal's baton upon the same day; and now the elder Prince was to see soldiering in earnest for the first time. But it was judged prudent not to send the future heir to the Prussian throne upon the ungrateful mission of repressing an internal revolt.

In October, upon completing his eighteenth year, Prince Frederick William came of age, according to precedent in the royal family of Prussia, and was solemnly invested with the Order of the Black Eagle, the highest Prussian order, which corresponds most nearly to the Garter in England. The young Prince's first quoted public utterance is the message in which he thanked the Municipality of Potsdam for their congratulations on this occasion: "I am still very young,' he said, 'but I will prepare myself with love and devotion for my high calling, and endeavour some day to fulfil these anticipations which will then become a duty entrusted to me by God.'

After a few months of service with his regiment, he left for the University of Bonn, attended by Colonel Fischer and an Aide-de-camp. It was a new departure, and typical of the changed order of ideas, that a Prince of the royal blood should enter as a student at a public university. The course of studies arranged for him formed no exception to the ordinary routine; and though he resided in the old Electoral Palace, his intercourse with the other students remained unrestricted; he attended the lectures of Dahlmann, Arndt, and Perthes, and completed his education in history, law, and literature. But his studies were not continued to the curriculum of the University. Mr. Copland Perry, who was at that time residing in Bonn, was invited to assist him in mastering the English language and literature. Mr. Perry writes: "At the Prince's request I attended on him three times a week, and had the honour of directing his studies of English history and literature, in which he took a very special interest. His love for England, and his profound admiration for our Queen, were most remarkable, and tended, of course, to render our intercourse the more interesting and confidential. Whatever information I was able to afford him about English political and social life was received by him with the greatest eagerness, and, when more solid study was concluded, we amused ourselves by writing imaginary letters to ministers and leaders of society.'

Shortly afterwards the Prince of Prussia, who was in 1849 appointed Military Governor of the Rhine Provinces and Westphalia, took up his residence at Coblenz. The reactionary policy of the Manteuffel Cabinet did not meet with his approval; he considered that the pledges of 1848 must be respected, and was glad to absent himself for a while from the Capital, where the gatherings of the Liberal chiefs and sympathizers at his palace were sure to attract attention. The visits of Prince Frederick William to Coblenz were frequent, and led to many acquaintances and conversations on social and political topics with the remarkable men the Princess of Prussia gathered round her Court. During his university career the area of his travels, which had hitherto been confined to German territory, was considerably extended. In 1850 he visited Switzerland, Northern Italy, and the South of France. The following year he accompanied his parents to England to witness the opening of the Great Exhibition. May-day, 1851, was a proud day for England. The continent had hardly recovered from the recent shocks of revolution; France, Austria, Germany, and the Italian States, had alike been torn by domestic strife, but in London all the nations of the earth had met together in friendly competition. The scheme had not passed without considerable opposition in England itself, but the energy and genius of the Prince Consort, the initiator of this international festival, had prevailed, and set an example which other nations would not be slow to follow. The young Prince, who also paid a hasty visit to Liverpool and to the Isle of Wight, carried back to Germany a deep impression of the wealth and stability of England, of the free spirit and reasonableness which governed her institutions, and above all a charming domestic picture of her happy Court, and of a little Princess, who was then just ten years old. He was, however, patriotic enough to say that he preferred Babelsberg to Windsor. Later in the year he accompanied his father on a visit to Russia, where he was appointed Honorary Colonel of the Eleventh Regiment of Hussars. He rejoined his regiment at Potsdam in time to take part in the Autumn Manoeuvres, and was advanced to the rank of Captain, returning soon afterwards to Bonn to conclude his university course.

At the university he first laid the foundation of that universal popularity which characterized the whole of his subsequent career. He succeeded in so merging the Prince in the student, that he was able to enter heart and soul into the spirit of university life. He had a word for everyone, and by those numerous excursions in the surrounding Rhineland, which, he so particularly appreciated, he had become a familiar figure in all the country side. It was a source of universal regret in Bonn, when, at Easter, 1852, the short space of time which could be spared from the Prince's busy life drew to its close, and town and university vied with one another in the ovations which marked his departure.

Returning to his regiment, the Prince devoted himself to military duties. He was now a Captain, and the personal interest which he took in each individual member of his company acquired him a proverbial popularity. During the Autumn Manoeuvres of 1853, when he was promoted to the rank of Major, he learned the duties of an Aide-de-camp, being attached to the Staff of Count V.J. Groeben, who at that time commanded the Corps of Guards. The Prince's life was one of constant activity: under General von Reyher he was instructed in the special branches of the Staff; while he found time to acquire a thorough knowledge of the working of the various civil departments, and devoted himself to the study of the internal administration, under the guidance of the Chief President of the Province of Brandenburg. During the Summer of this year he had accompanied his father to the Manoeuvres of the Austrian Army, and was assigned by the Emperor Franz Joseph the honorary command of the Twentieth Regiment of Infantry. About this period he was also initiated into the mysteries of Freemasonry, and the Prince of Prussia, who had taken this influential Order under his protection, availed himself of the occasion to protest, in his speech, against the attempt made by a certain section in the country, to cast discredit on this ancient institution. In December he had an attack of inflammation of the lungs, and after his recovery it was considered advisable for him to spend a Winter in the South, and thus, a long cherished plan of a tour in Italy was carried into effect.

The royal party were conveyed from Trieste to Ancona in an Austrian man of war, and proceeded thence direct to Home. The old Papal Court was then in all its brilliancy, and Rome was still the city of Corinne and Transformation. No lines of railway pierced the circuit of her walls, there was no gas in the narrow alleys, but the quaint old gilded coaches of the Cardinals, the gay uniforms of the Papal troops, the numberless religious orders, the costume of the people, which was then not confined to professional models and beggars, filled her streets with colour, and the Carnival was still a national fête. Italian Unity had assuredly no warmer sympathizer than Prince Frederick William, but the Rome of his impressions never ceased to be an interesting and charming recollection. He was repeatedly received with every mark of appreciation by Pope Pius IX, who preserved a warm regard for his royal guest, which the grave issues of later years between Prussia and the Vatican in no way diminished, and he assisted at the Consistory in which the present Pontiff received the Cardinal's Hat. The story is told that at their first interview the Pope held out his hand to the young Prince for the customary kiss of homage, but the latter, as representative of one of the two great Protestant States, did not feel called upon to render this salute, and warmly grasped the extended hand. The Pope, whose sense of humour was well known, always at subsequent interviews greeted the young Prince on entering with his hand behind his back. The journey was extended to Naples and Sicily, and the royal party returned to Rome on their way northward to witness the Easter ceremonies.

After six months' service with the Artillery, Prince Frederick William was transferred to the Dragoons of the Guard. It may be well here to explain that the Guards form an entire army corps, including, therefore, infantry, artillery, and cavalry of every arm; they are distributed between Berlin, Potsdam, and the neighbouring fortress of Spandau. The infantry regiment to which the Prince was first attached is quartered in Potsdam; the Dragoons of the Guard, consisting then of one regiment only, but now of two, are stationed in Berlin.

Colonel von Griesheim, an old friend of the Prince of Prussia, who commanded the regiment, has left a record of an interview which he had with the Princess, at the time they entrusted their son to his care. The Princess, he says, begged him in no way to spare his new officer, but to let him enter into every detail of duty, in order that he might really learn to appreciate the hard work which military service entailed. She bade him never lose sight of the fact that he was to teach his future Sovereign, and that it was essential to his forming a just appreciation of things, that he should see their working side. The Prince of Prussia, who came in at the close of the interview, said, with a smile, 'I taught him his business, and now he is to teach our son!'

The Colonel most conscientiously carried out his trust, and the Prince entered upon the routine of his duties as Captain. The riding lessons, the horse-breaking, the stable drill, the gymnastic courses, the stores of his squadron, were all handed over to his personal control and management, and so quickly and practically did he master the duties of a cavalry officer, that on the 31st August, 1855, he was appointed to command the regiment. About this time an officer, who has since been somewhat talked of, was appointed Aide-de-camp to the Prince; a man of few words, but striking lucidity of expression and determination of character, and an enthusiastic lover of music, whose age was just that of the century. His name was Colonel von Moltke, and he was at the time Chief of the Staff of the Fourth Army Corps.

During the Summer of 1855, the Prince went for a second time to England. Perhaps on the occasion of his former visit, four years previously, a plan had already suggested itself to him which he now determined to realize, of asking the hand of the Princess Royal in marriage. At any rate he now expressed a wish to visit the Queen and the Prince Consort, who invited him to stay at Balmoral; and on the 20th of September the Prince Consort wrote to his old friend and confidant, Baron Stockmar, to tell him that the proposal, made with the concurrence of the King, as well as of the Prince of Prussia, had been accepted, subject, of course, to the consent of the Princess Royal herself, from whom, he added, he did not anticipate any hesitation. It was, however, not to be broken to her till after her Confirmation in the following Spring, and the marriage was on no account to take place until the Princess had passed her seventeenth birthday. But with all these excellent dispositions the natural impatience of the Prince prevailed, and on the 29th of September, when the royal party were riding unattended over the moors, a spray of the rare white heather, which the Prince dismounted to pluck and offer to his future bride, drew the secret from his lips, and the happy alliance was arranged, not by the manoeuvring of diplomacy or the scheming of politicians, but naturally, and as in the everyday world, by the spontaneous impulse of two young hearts towards each other.

On his return to Bonn the Prince unburdened his heart to Mr Perry, whom he had from the outset treated with the greatest confidence, and to whom he had spoken of his hope of winning the hand of the Princess Royal. 'It was not politics,' he said, 'it was not ambition; it was my heart.'

On the 2nd of October the Prince Consort wrote to Baron Stockmar: 'Prince Frederick William left us yesterday .... The young people are genuinely in love with one another: the guilelessness, simplicity, and

unselfishness of the young man are quite touching ....
We are quite unprepared for any public
announcement of the marriage at present. The secret
must be kept *tout bien que mal*.' But the secret leaked
out, as such secrets always do; the visits of the future
Sovereign of Prussia were too significant to be
disregarded.

The engagement of Princess Louise to the Prince
Regent, now the reigning Grand Duke of Baden, took
place on the same day, September 29, at Coblenz.
The following year the Prince returned to England, in
May, where he was joined shortly afterwards by his
future brother-in-law, and the two Princes received
honorary degrees from the University of Oxford, and
were present at the festivities of Commemoration. In
August he was for the first time entrusted with a public
mission, and sent to represent the King at Moscow, at
the coronation of the Emperor Alexander II, who had
succeeded his father in the previous year. On all these
journeys he was accompanied by his new Aide-de-
camp, who was about this time promoted to the rank
of Major-General. The latter has testified in his
correspondence to the remarkable natural tact and
the happy faculty of the *apropos* displayed by the
Prince in meeting and conversing with the number of
notabilities who were here for the first time presented
to him.

On the 20th of September the marriage of Princess
Louise with the Grand Duke of Baden took place, and
shortly afterwards Prince Frederick William received
the command of the Eleventh Regiment of Infantry,
which forms part of the garrison of Breslau, in Silesia.
He had some time previously returned from his short
term of service with the Cavalry, to the First Infantry
of the Guards, and qualified himself to take command

of the regiment. No sooner, however, had the Prince taken up his quarters at Breslau, than another journey to England was determined on, and the visit, whose ostensible object was to congratulate the Princess upon her birthday, extended over a month. He returned by Paris, where he was most warmly received by the Emperor Napoleon III and the Empress Eugenie. A letter from the latter describing the visit is not without its curious interest, read in the light of subsequent events. 'The Prince is a tall, finely proportioned man, nearly a head taller than the Emperor, smart, fair, with light yellow moustache, a German, as Tacitus describes them, chivalrous in manner, and with a touch of Hamlet about him. His companion, a General Moltke, is a gentleman of few words, but nothing less than a dreamer; always attentive and commanding attention, he surprises you by the most striking observations. An imposing race, these Germans. Louis says, the race of the future. But we have not got to that yet.'

Prince Frederick William remained with his regiment in Silesia until September, 1857, finding time, however, in the Summer for another visit to England. It was originally contemplated that the marriage should take place this year, but the health of King Frederick William IV., who had for some time been ailing, gave rise to considerable anxiety, and it was decided to postpone it for a while. At length the malady, which had affected the brain, was declared to be incurable, and on the 23rd of October the Prince of Prussia was named Regent for three months. This term was subsequently prolonged from time to time, and in the following year, when the King left Berlin for Italy, the Prince Regent assumed the full responsibility of government, which he retained until that Monarch's death. The marriage was now definitively fixed for January 25, 1858.

It was with sincere regret that Prince Frederick
William took leave of the officers and men of his
Silesian regiment. Silesia is the favourite province of
the kingdom; the wealthiest and most influential of
the Prussian nobility have their country seats there;
the forests offer great attractions to the sportsman;
and Breslau itself is within easy distance of the
pleasant country sloping upwards to the giant
mountains which mark the boundary of Bohemia.
Besides, he had greatly appreciated the freedom of life
which his sojourn here had permitted, and was much
attached to and beloved by the regiment had
commanded. The close of his farewell speech was
remembered a few years later, when, in the campaign
of '66, he was entrusted with the command of the
Second Army, and with orders to protect the province
of Silesia: 'I shall never forget these days, nor you,' he
said; 'and my ardent desire, which it would give me
the greatest joy to see accomplished, is that I may
some day receive with you - who are, for the most
part, my pupils - the baptism of blood before the
enemy.'

Meanwhile, the day fixed for the wedding
ceremony drew near. On the 23rd of January, Prince
Frederick William arrived in England to claim his
bride. London had been already several days *en fête*.
On the evening of the 23rd there was a State
performance at Her Majesty's Theatre, where the
Prince was, for the first time, present during the
festival proceedings, sitting beside the Princess Royal;
and rarely has London witnessed such an enthusiastic
scene. The singing of the National Anthem was the
signal for a burst of cheering, to which the Queen
graciously responded. A cry of 'Princess' then rang

throughout the house. The Queen beckoned the Princess Royal to the front of the box, and there she curtseyed her acknowledgments amidst a display of feeling which made the pretty episode for ever memorable. The wedding took place at the Chapel Royal, St. James's, on the following Monday. The accounts of the ceremony, read in the light and shadow of all that has passed since, are eminently touching from the genuine and natural feeling evinced, and an eye-witness, describing the scene as the procession left the Chapel Royal, wrote: 'The light of happiness in the eyes of the bride appealed to the most reserved among the spectators, and an audible '*God bless you!*' passed from mouth to mouth along the line.' The details of the ceremony, recorded by a loving hand in the Queen's diary, and published in Sir Theodore Martin's *Life of the Prince Consort*, are too well-known to call for reproduction here. It shall only be mentioned that the wedding rings were made of pure Silesian gold, and that the eight bridesmaids - chosen from the fairest daughters of England - wore the emblematic white heather, in memory of the stranger-Prince's wooing. Throughout the country in England the day was celebrated as a national holiday by public rejoicings and free dinners to the poor; and in the evening London was a blaze of illuminations, for the match had become thoroughly popular. Parliament had met the proposed vote with scarcely a dissentient voice; and the young Prince had won a place in the heart of the nation, which learned to appreciate him ever more and more as time went on.

The short honeymoon was spent at Windsor, and the departure was fixed for the second of February. The farewell procession left Buckingham Palace, and proceeded by the Strand, St. Paul's, and London Bridge, to the station in the Kent Road, where the

49

royal party were to take the train for Gravesend. The Prince Consort, with his two eldest sons, accompanied Prince Frederick William and his bride, while the Queen watched from the balcony of Buckingham Palace till the procession wound out of sight. The snow was falling fast, but they drove in open carriages to see the last of home. Every point of vantage along the route was filled to overflowing, and it seemed as if the whole nation felt keenly the sense of parting, and had come out in its thousands to speed on her way, with their love and kindly solicitude, one who, though still almost a child, was leaving her country for ever, to make her home in an alien land. It is a solemn moment, hard to realize for those who stay at home, that in which we turn our backs for ever on the only life we have known, and go to meet the untried and the new, to dwell with strange faces, different ideas and ideals, unfamiliar associations.

At Gravesend, the royal yacht, *Victoria and Albert*, was waiting to receive them; and the closing scene in England was thus described in *The Times* of the 23rd of February: -

'In compliance with injunctions issued just before the arrival of the royal party, there was little cheering on the pier itself. Still, however, it could not altogether prevent the cheers which greeted the bride, as she stood leaning on her husband's arm …. Her royal husband was, of course, received with a most marked welcome, which he seemed to feel; though, as usual, he always left his bride to receive the ovations offered, and watched her every movement 'with the most affectionate solicitude.

'On the affecting farewell we need not dwell. Every heart can sympathize with them, not as rulers or princes, but as a father who parts from his eldest child - 'with young brothers, who see their sister leave them for the first time, to cast her lot for ever in a land of strangers. The Prince Consort was grave, but composed, though the effort it cost him to maintain an appearance of serenity was visible to all. With less self-command, the Prince of Wales and Prince Alfred made little attempt to conceal their grief .... As the paddles went round, the quick flashes of broad red flame through the snowstorm, followed by the sullen boom of cannon, showed that old Tilbury was at last saluting for the departure. The Prince Consort waved his hand to the Royal Bridegroom again and again, but kept his composure; but not so did the young Princes, whose grief seemed only redoubled by the tokens of farewell round them. Neither could conceal his sorrow, and neither tried to do so, but stood brushing away the tears from their eyes .... On such an occasion there was not many who could resist the contagious influence of a sorrow so innocent and so sincere, and there were few who looked with dry eyes on this departure of the daughter of England.'

The marriage of Prince Frederick William of Prussia and Victoria, Princess Royal, 1858, detail from a painting by John Phillip

III.

1858 — 1863.

THE bride and bridegroom's journey home was one long triumphal progress. At Herbesthal, where the German frontier was first reached, Count Kedern awaited them with a message of welcome from the King, At Aix-la-Chapelle; at Cologne, where they halted for the night; at Hanover, where they alighted to pay a brief visit to the King; at Magdeburg, where a second night was passed, deputations were awaiting to receive them - triumphal arches and illuminations testified the enthusiasm and loyalty of the populations. A brilliant reception was prepared for them at Potsdam, where they arrived on the 6th February; and the following day, a Sunday, was devoted to rest after their eventful journey. On Monday, the 8th, the solemn entry into the capital took place. The sixteen miles from Potsdam to the capital were traversed by road. At the Bellevue Palace, situated in the Thiergarten, or park, about a mile from the Brandenburg Gate, the King was waiting to greet his nephew and niece. After a short interval the procession reformed, the bells rang, the canons fired salutes, and the state coach, drawn by eight horses, arrived at the Brandenburg Gate. Here the royal pair were welcomed in the name of the garrison by the venerable Field-Marshal, Count Wrangel. A detachment of the Life Guards rode before and after the carriage; while the Prince's old regiment, the Dragoons of the Guard, formed the rest of the escort. Forty out-riders and deputations from the various Guilds headed the procession; and so, between a surging mass of spectators, they passed down the Linden Avenue, the whole length of which was hung with British and Prussian flags to the old palace and its eastern extremity, where the Prince of Prussia was waiting to receive them at the foot of the great staircase. After the ceremonial introductions had been made, the Prince and Princess appeared on the balcony, to receive the homage of the people, and watch the Guilds march past. In the evening they drove through the city, where there was not a window unilluminated, and no house so poor that it had not some decoration in honour of the festal day. It was still hard Winter in the northern city, but its welcome was warm and generous.

After a short residence in the old Schloss, a palace in the Linden Avenue, close to the opera house, and facing the arsenal, which had been enlarged and restored for King Frederick William III, was assigned to the young couple, where they took up their abode in the early Winter, and ever after, as Crown Prince and Princess, continued to live when in Berlin. The first Summer was spent at the Prince of Prussia's country seat of Babelsberg, the home of Prince Frederick William's boyhood; and here, at Whitsuntide, they received a hasty visit from the Prince Consort, who returned in August with the Queen. This visit, the bright impression left by which is fully recorded in the Queen's diary, was the only one which Her Majesty was able to pay her daughter in her new home, until the sad and memorable journey of this year, when the shadow of death was already darkening its threshold, and the streets of the capital were still draped with black in mourning for the first German Emperor.

An heir to the Hohenzollern dynasty was born on the 27th of January, 1859 - the reigning Emperor, William II. The apartments at Babelsberg now became too small for the extended requirements of the young household, and from henceforth the New Palace, near Potsdam, became their Summer home. And here it was that the Crown Princess, as she soon afterwards came to be called, was able to set the example of that helpful and happy country life which she had learned in England to value, so that it was not long before its simple domestic character became proverbial, and exercised a far-reaching influence. Under her fostering hand, the old formal pleasure-grounds and the neglected gardens became a pattern of taste and arrangement. In their neighbouring farm of Bornstedt the Prince himself superintended every detail, and taught himself the management of land and labour, while the dairy and the poultry-yard were the particular care of the Princess. All the inhabitants of the neighbouring villages quickly learned to appreciate their kindly solicitude; the sanitation of dwellings, the care for the sick and aged among their tenants, the schools, the children's holidays, all engaged their sympathetic interest. One of the Prince's most striking characteristics was his love for the people, his genuine sympathy with the humbler walks of life. It was his especial pleasure to visit the village school and listen to the children's lessons, and sometimes he would take the teacher's place and put the questions himself. It must have been on such an occasion that the pretty reply was given which is recorded in the following story: - 'To what kingdom does this belong?' the Prince had enquired of a little girl, touching a medal suspended to his chain. 'To the mineral kingdom,' was the answer. 'And this?' pointing to a flower. 'To the vegetable kingdom.' 'And I myself,' he asked; 'to what kingdom do I belong?' 'To the kingdom of heaven,' was the child's reply.

Meanwhile, there were duties, and important ones, to perform. On the day of his marriage the Prince had been promoted to the rank of Major-General, and when, during the Austrian and Italian war of 1859, it was determined to mobilize a portion of the Prussian troops, he was appointed to command the First Infantry Division, an appointment confirmed and made definite on the 25th of July. The Peace of Villafranca brought the war to an abrupt conclusion before the Prussian mobilization was complete, but the experience had revealed serious defects in the existing state of the Army, and a Commission was immediately organized to consider the remodelling of the entire military system. The Prince assisted at all the deliberations of this Commission, and after its sittings were closed he started with the Princess for a tour in Silesia, and, later, paid a hasty visit to London.

The following year a daughter was born, Princess Charlotte, now Hereditary Princess of Saxe-Meiningen. It was in the late Summer of this year that the Queen and the Prince Consort paid their last visit together to Germany. During their stay at Coburg their first grandchild, the little Prince William, was brought by his parents to be shown to his grandparents. A charming picture is given in the Queen's diary of the first appearance of the present German Emperor 'in a little white dress with black bows.'

The measures of reform in the military system, which the Prince Regent held to be urgent and indispensable, led to protracted discussion, and eventually to the resignation of the Liberal Ministry. The question was still undecided when, on the 2nd of January, 1861, King Frederick William IV died, and the Prince Regent ascended the throne under the name of King William I. Prince Frederick William, who had in the previous year been promoted to the rank of Lieutenant-General, now assumed the title of Crown Prince. The Coronation took place with much pomp at Königsberg, on his birthday, the 18th of October. He was on this occasion named Protector of the ancient University of Königsberg, as successor to the late King; and shortly afterwards, in accordance with precedent, was appointed Stadtholder of Pomerania, though the formal announcement did not appear in the Gazette till the following year, on the birthday of Prince William, the reigning Emperor, when it was couched in these terms: - 'I have appointed your Royal Highness to be Stadtholder of Pomerania, and desire thus to mark the day, on which so happy an event in the history of our family is commemorated, by an especial token of my fatherly affection. - William.'

Early in the married life of the Crown Prince and Princess fell the shadow of those domestic sorrows which darkened so many of their years. On March 16th, 1861, the Duchess of Kent died; and the loss of 'this much-loved grandmother' was soon to be followed by a still nearer and more untimely bereavement. It was not long after the festivities of the Coronation that the health of the Prince Consort began to give cause for anxiety. It had been his special desire that the Crown Princess, who had herself been suffering in health, should not expose herself to the risk of a Winter journey, and she was therefore not present at that sad event which has cast a permanent gloom over the British Court.[1] Needless to say, the Crown Prince crossed to England immediately, to be of such service as he might, and to attend the funeral of one to whom he had looked up with fond affection; a guide and a counsellor, whose moderation and political foresight he never ceased to regard with respect and veneration. Some months later, in the Spring of the following year, he was once more in England, to attend, at the special desire of the Queen, the opening of the second great International Exhibition, for which he was Prussian Commissioner. A few days afterwards he was the guest of the Royal Academy at their annual banquet, and in his speech on that occasion he naturally referred to the loss which had cast a gloom over the festivities, and recalled the debt that was owed to the initiator of those international gatherings which have done so much to promote the interests of commerce, and, by teaching the nations to know one another better, have so largely contributed to their peace and welfare. This speech, which later on in the evening was characterized by Lord Granville as 'a speech remarkable for its simple and truthful eloquence, and which, by a touch of feeling concerning one of whom this country is proud, went directly to our hearts,' was as follows : -

'SIR CHARLES EASTLAKE,[2] YOUR ROYAL HIGHNESS, MY LORDS AND GENTLEMEN, - I hope that the gratitude which I feel for the cordiality with which you have been pleased to propose and receive my health will not be measured by the manner in which I return thanks for it, as I am sorry to say I fear

I shall not be able to express my feelings as I should perhaps be able to do were I longer accustomed to the language of this dear country. I thank you first for the way in which you have been kind enough to speak of my near relationship to the Royal Family of England; nor can I on such an occasion omit referring to the loss which this country has recently sustained - a loss felt so intimately by your Royal Family and also by my own. We have all heard from the President how that loss has been felt here, and I am happy to say that in my own country the same monumental feeling will always remain associated with the memory of that dear Prince who was taken so suddenly' from us.

'It is not necessary for me to say how happy I am to be able to be present at this great festival of peace, and at the same time to honour the great undertaking which we owe to the master-mind of him I was so proud to regard as my father-in-law. I have also, Sir Charles, to thank you for the manner in which you spoke just now of the state of Art and Science in my own country, and especially of the articles sent to the Great International Exhibition. I am happy to think, from the way in which that reference of the President was received, that you all appear to agree with him on that point, and 1 hope I can say that the same feeling for English art is reciprocated by my country. Perhaps I may be allowed to say, as I am proud to say, that the Princess Royal of your country is one of the first representatives of English art in my country. Returning thanks again for the kind way in which I have been received, I can only add that I hope it will be a new tie, strengthening those warm sympathies I have always felt for this great country; and, more than this, that the strong sympathy which always existed in my own heart will in Prussia and the great Fatherland of Germany be more and more, and for ever, retained.'[3]

No mean achievement in a foreign tongue. Among the guests at this Academy banquet, of which the Crown Prince ever preserved a pleasant recollection, were Thackeray and Dickens, the latter of whom responded on behalf of Literature.

A few months later, the Crown Prince was again at Königsberg, where he was solemnly invested with the office of High Protector of the University, which he had consented to fill at the time of the Coronation. His speech on this occasion must also be quoted, for in it the aims and aspirations which were ever nearest to his heart found expression:

'I looked upon the inheritance to which I have succeeded as a renewed invitation to contribute my aid to the development of Art and Science. That which my ancestors have established and honourably maintained will be sacred no less to me their successor; and I promise, on my part, to support and extend the establishment by all the means in my power. I have in my mind those great names which have made this University illustrious - above all, the name of one man, whose teachings have gone forth far over the bounds of our German Fatherland, and have enlightened the whole round world.[4] I have myself been a member of an University, and I know the spirit by which it is animated. The work of the Universities - the development of the mind and the strengthening of character - is a noble work, in that they fulfil this mission, not only for the advancement of learning, but in the service of the State. Thanks to the spirit which fires the youth of Germany, I count upon her students understanding and appreciating the greatness of this work.'

During this Summer, there was consolation in the house of mourning; a second son was born, Prince Henry, who has become the sailor-Prince of Germany. In the meanwhile, the conflict between the Government and the Chambers had continued, and was now assuming a more acute phase, when in September, 1862, the King called upon Herr von Bismarck to take the reins of Government in hand.

From this period began for Prussia that wonderful career of success, the extraordinary decade which culminated with the declaration of the German Empire at Versailles. Of the relation of the Crown Prince to political life it does not enter into the design of the present sketch to speak; but it may here be placed on record that through the quarter of a century which followed, he never broke the rule he had laid down for himself to refrain from any open expression of opinion, and from taking any active part in political life. Differences of opinion there must always be, and the younger generation is not always patient of the views and methods of the older. But whatever may have been the feelings and sentiments of the Crown Prince himself, he cheerfully and loyally carried out the arduous duties which it fell to him to perform; and, at a subsequent date, when called upon for a time to assume the Regency, he faithfully followed in the lines that were laid down for him. It argues no slight strength of character, and a paramount sense of duty, to have so faithfully appreciated and conquered the difficulties of the position which it was his lot to fill.

The Crown Prince and the Princess spent the Winter months of this year in a long tour through Italy, during which an improvised expedition was made to Tunis and Malta. They had joined the Prince of Wales on the Royal yacht *Osborne,* and at Naples celebrated his coming of age on board, returning subsequently to Rome, where they took up their abode in the Palazzo Cafiarelli.

Prince and Princess Frederick William of Prussia, c.1860

Crown Prince and Princess Frederick William of Prussia, 1863

IV.

1864 — 1869.

WHEN the Danish War broke out in 1864 the Crown Prince had no military command, but was attached to the Staff of Field-Marshal Count von Wrangel, who had the chief command of the united Austrian and Prussian armies. His task was to be one of conciliation. The allied armies were the allies of circumstance rather than of sympathy, and the rivalry of the commanding officers, the jealousy of the troops, could hardly fail to produce a feeling of friction which might, if not counteracted with tact and authority, have prejudiced the prospects of the campaign. In all such differences and disputes the Crown Prince formed the court of reference, and the fact that the cessation of hostilities was so soon afterwards followed by the outbreak of the Austrian and Prussian War proves how difficult must have been the task imposed upon him, and how effectual was the influence of his tact and judgment in preventing these disagreements from assuming an acute phase before the war was brought to a successful conclusion. At a skirmish before Düppel he was for the first time under fire, and he assisted at the storming of the lines of Düppel on the 18th of April,

1864. Throughout the severe Winter campaign he shared every hardship with the troops; he was continually in their midst, and the sight of his familiar figure, in the long military paletot, with his short pipe in his mouth, was a signal for general enthusiasm. It was now that the Crown Prince, in co-operation with the Crown Princess, who had gone to meet him at Hamburg as soon as the fighting was over, founded the first of those institutions for the relief of the victims of war, of which many were called into existence later, in the stormy days which were yet in store for Prussia. After the conclusion of Peace the Crown Prince was entrusted with the command of the Second Army Corps, which he retained until the war of 1870. On the 11th of September of the same year Prince Sigismund was born, 'a great source of rejoicing to his parents.' The history of the family of Hohenzollern is full of strange coincidences, but perhaps there are few stranger than that connected with the brief life of this little Prince, ushered into the world after the declaration of peace, with the Emperor of Austria for his godfather, to be taken away once more, almost on the very day his native land had drawn the sword against Austria.

The interval of peace was short. Since the Italian war of 1859 the relations between Austria and Prussia had continued strained, and the Danish campaign had only served to widen the breach. The struggle for the hegemony of the German Confederation was at hand. Austria realized at length that Prussia was in deadly earnest, and meant not only to oust her from the headship she still claimed, but from the confederation altogether; and long before appeal was made to the decision of the sword, rumours of war were rife, and hostile preparations continued. In May, 1866, the Prussian army was mobilized. The fighting strength of the kingdom was divided into three armies, of which the second was placed under the command of the Crown Prince, with orders to protect the province of Silesia, of which he was appointed Military Governor during the mobilization.

So long as war still hung in the balance, the Crown Prince used his influence on the side of conciliation, and did all that was in his power to avert a conflict. Now that it appeared inevitable, he was as ever ready to do his duty. A few days after the christening of his second daughter, who, having been baptized on the 24th of May, received the name of Victoria, he rejoined his Staff at Breslau; and, as the veteran generals gathered round him, he said, with his genial smile: 'It really is too bad that so young a man as I am should command you, with all your experience, and I with none myself.' On the 14th of June the Prussian proposals were rejected in the Diet at Frankfort; Hanover and Hesse fell almost without a struggle, before the iron will of the great minister, and the dogs of war were loosed. The day after the issue of the Royal Proclamation to the Army, the Crown Prince addressed his troops from his headquarters at Neisse: -

'SOLDIERS OF THE SECOND ARMY,

'You have heard the words of our King and Commander-in-Chief. The efforts of His Majesty to preserve peace for our country have been vain. With a heavy heart, but relying on the devotion and bravery of his army, the King has resolved to fight for the honour and independence of Prussia, and for the effectual reorganization of Germany.

'Placed at your head by the grace of my royal

father, and thanks to the confidence he reposes in me, I am proud, as our King's first subject, to stake my life with you for all that our fatherland holds most sacred.

'Soldiers! For the first time in the last fifty years our army has to face a foe that is its equal match. Have confidence in your strength, in the efficiency of your arms, and remember we have now got to beat the same enemy whom our greatest King once vanquished with a little army.

'And now forward, under the old Prussian device, 'With God for king and country!'

The Crown Prince had left for the campaign under very painful circumstances, for a few days before his departure. Prince Sigismund, 'a beautiful boy, the joy and pride of his Parents,' was taken very ill. Even the doctor who had attended him was summoned to the front by the fate of war, and the Crown Princess was left alone with her sick child. The illness, which was at first difficult to recognize, assumed a fatal form,[1] and on the 18th of June the little Prince succumbed, leaving his mother well-nigh distracted and alone, without anyone to share her sorrow. The news reached the Crown Prince just as the army was on the point of advancing. He had with him one tried and trusted friend, Captain Mischke, a companion of his early days, and it was his warm sympathy on which the Crown Princess relied to help her husband at this critical moment to bear so hard and crushing a blow.

There were perhaps many others in the camp who had their silent troubles; such things must always be. It is not the least of the terrors of war, that, when the summons comes, the claims of home and the affections of the individual must yield to the general welfare; but it may have encouraged some of those who stood in like case to see how bravely and unswervingly their leader went about his duty, never allowing his private griefs for a moment to divert his energies from the grave task he had in hand. Those who knew him well were aware how acutely he suffered, but it was only after the war was over, in a speech made to the Municipality of Berlin, when tendering their congratulations on his safe return, that he spoke of his personal loss: 'It was a heavy trial,' he said, 'to be separated from my wife and my dying boy; that I could not be there to close his eyes. Hard as it was at the time to have to be far from my home and family, I can now look back upon it with satisfaction, for it was a sacrifice which I offered to my country.'

The force commanded by the Crown Prince consisted of four army corps; the first under General von Bonin, the fifth under General von Steinmetz, who was commander of the First Army in the war of 1870, the sixth under General von Mutius, and the Corps of the Guards, under Prince August of Württemberg. He was supported by an able adviser in the person of General von Blumenthal, who acted as Chief of the Staff. General von Blumenthal accompanied the Prince in the same capacity during the Franco-German war, and one of the few public acts of his brief reign was to bestow a field-marshal's baton on his old friend and faithful servant, for whose military capacity and private character he had unbounded esteem, which it was his especial pleasure to express whenever he had an opportunity.

The instructions issued by General von Moltke, who as chief of the head-quarter Staff directed the operations of the three armies, were: to enter

Bohemia through the passes of the Giant Mountains, and effect a junction with the armies of Prince Frederick Charles and General Herwarth. A wide latitude was however left to the judgment and initiative of the commander, and it was pointed out that, if their concentration was not yet effected, circumstances might admit of a series of attacks in overwhelming force on isolated bodies of the enemy, which might modify the scheme of campaign. The junction of the armies in the direction of Gitschin was however still to be the ultimate object, and the relative positions of the three armies was ever to be kept in sight, with a view to mutual support. This forecast was carried out in its double event. Four Austrian corps operating independently opposed the invading Prussians; with the exception of a slight check experienced by General von Bonin on the 27th, a series of rapid successes between the 26th and 28th cleared the way into Bohemia, and on the 30th the three advancing Prussian corps re-united with the sixth, which had formed the rearguard. On the 1st of July the Crown Prince issued the following' proclamation: -

'Only a few days have elapsed since we crossed the Bohemian frontier, and a series of brilliant victories has marked our advance, and ensured the attainment of our first object, to hold the passages of the Elbe, and unite with the First Army.

'The gallant Fifth Army Corps, under its heroic leader (General v. Steinmetz), has gloriously repulsed on three successive days as many fresh bodies of the enemy advancing against them. The Guards have been twice engaged, and have brilliantly succeeded in beating the enemy back. The First Army Corps has displayed the greatest bravery under the most trying circumstances.

'Five flags, two standards, 8,000 prisoners have fallen into our hands, and many thousands of killed and wounded, are evidence of how severe the losses of the enemy have been.

'We have to mourn the loss of many gallant comrades, killed or wounded, who have made a gap in our ranks. But the thought of having fallen for their King and their country, together with the consciousness of victory, will have afforded consolation to the dying and comfort to the suffering.

'God grant that we may continue in our career of victory!

'I thank the generals, officers, and men of the Second Army for their gallantry in battle, and for their patience in surmounting the great difficulties we have had to encounter, and I feel proud to command such troops.'

But the hardest struggle was yet to come. The First Army and the Army of the Elbe had also in the meantime entered Bohemia, and after a series of successes had converged upon Gitschin, the point at which the three armies were to effect their union. The King arrived at Gitschin on the 2nd of July to take over the supreme command. It was decided that the troops should enjoy a short rest before the decisive engagement with the forces of General Benedek, now concentrated in the neighbourhood of Königgrätz; but a message from Prince Frederick Charles, who was not aware of the full strength of General Benedek's army, that he should attack the Austrian position on the following morning, relying on the support of the Second Anny and the Army of the Elbe, changed these dispositions, and the general attack was ordered for the 3rd. The Crown Prince's army was still some fourteen miles from Gitschin, and on the night of the 2nd orders were despatched for his immediate advance. On the safe delivery of these orders hung the issue of the day. An hour after midnight, Count Finkenstein started on his eventful ride through the enemy's country, while a second instruction was forwarded by a safe and more circuitous route. At a quarter past three on the morning of the third he reached the bivouack of the advance guard of the Second Army, and warned General von Bonin to be prepared. By four in the morning the message was safely delivered at headquarters, and by daybreak the columns were advancing without train or baggage, straining every nerve to reach the field in time. The Crown Prince rode at their head, urging and encouraging his men, as they heard in the distance the thunder of the cannon of Sadowa growing nearer and nearer. The Prussians were heavily outnumbered in the morning, and victory hung in the scales. The Austrians fought, as ever, with the utmost bravery and determination, and had the Crown Prince reached the battlefield a little later the whole issue of the war might have been changed. But it was only one o'clock when the artillery of the Second Army opened fire upon the Austrian right, by two o'clock the whole army was engaged, and General von Moltke, turning to the King, said, 'Now, no power on earth can take the victory from your Majesty.' It was the forced march of the Second Army that won the decisive battle of Sadowa. The Austrians lost in killed, wounded, and prisoners, upwards of 40,000 men, while the rest of their army was in full retreat over the Elbe or into the fortress of Königgrätz.

It was late in the evening before the Crown Prince found his father. Their meeting is thus recorded in his diary: 'At last, after much questioning and searching, we met the King; I reported to him the presence of my army on the field of battle, and kissed his hand, and he embraced me. For a time neither of us could find words. At last he said that he was rejoiced at my successes, and that I had shown aptitude for command. He had conferred on me, as I would know by telegraph, the Order 'le Mérite.' I had not received this telegram; and so my father and Sovereign bestowed upon me, on the field of a battle which I had assisted in winning, our highest Order of military distinction. I was deeply moved, and those who assisted at the interview seemed to share my emotion.'

The interview was thus also briefly described by the King in a letter written on the following morning to the Queen. 'At last I met Fritz with his Staff, quite late, at eight o'clock. What a moment after all we had gone through, and on the evening of such a day! I gave him myself the Order 'Pour le Mérite.' Tears started from his eyes, for he had not received my telegram announcing it. It was a complete surprise.'

The Order 'Pour le Mérite' is so highly esteemed, because it can only be won for personal gallantry upon the field of battle, and it had an especial value for the Prince to whom so many decorations had fallen ex officio, in being the one Order which had to be earned. By the express desire of the Emperor William, this Order, which he had won himself in 1815, was hung round his neck after death, and buried with him.

The war was not over, but there was little more

fighting for the Second Army to do. The Prussian troops pressed on to within sight of Vienna, and on the 26th of July preliminaries of peace were signed at Nikolsburg. The Treaty of Prague, signed in the following month, prepared the way for the unity of Germany. The immediate results were that the Sovereign of Prussia, whose territories had now been extended by the annexation of Hanover, Hesse, Schleswig-Holstein, Nassau, and Frankfort, became President of a new North German Confederation, including all the States of Northern and Central Germany, with absolute control of their military organization, while offensive and defensive alliances with the States and Southern Germany placed at his disposal the whole available fighting strength of the German nation.

Such were the momentous changes effected by the brief but brilliant campaign of 1866, to whose success the Crown Prince had so largely contributed. As he drove into Berlin beside the King, on the 4th of August, and the people closed in round the carriage with cheer on cheer, he may well have felt a thrill of conscious pride at having so fully justified the high command with which he had been entrusted. The glory of the successful soldier is still man's fondest ambition; we had nearly all of us rather have been Caesar than Socrates. But the scenes of the last weeks had left a dark impression on the quick sensibilities and the gentle nature of the soldier-Prince, which the flush of triumph could not altogether efface, and he had seen upon what narrow issues the fate of battles hung. There was still much more of this rough work for him to do, inevitable for the Prince as for the Private. But his inmost feelings are revealed in a few words which he made use of sometime afterwards in the course of conversation, when the Luxembourg

74

question was agitating the public mind, and the danger of hostilities was again within measurable distance. 'You have never seen war,' he said to one who had lightly spoken of its probability, 'or you would never pronounce that word so calmly. I, who have been brought face to face with war, must tell you that it is a paramount duty to avoid it, if it be possible. To make war is to incur a terrible responsibility. A statesman, even when he foresees the necessity of war, ought not to provoke it by artificial means, unless he be a genius and is confident of success. Otherwise he is tempting God. On the other hand, to await the contingency of war with firmness, and not to shrink from it if it is forced upon one, is the duty of a man. In acting so, we shall have public opinion and Heaven on our side.'

After the war of 1866 the Crown Prince rejoined the Crown Princess in Heringsdorf, a little village on the shores of the Baltic, to which the Princess and her children had retired on account of the cholera, which was then very bad in Potsdam. Thence they proceeded to Admannsdorf, in Silesia, not far from the Bohemian frontier, where the Princess occupied herself in tending the wounded soldiers, both Prussian and Austrian.

And now once more it fell to his lot to undertake the task of conciliation, and to gain the attachment of the new provinces; and as he travelled from one to the other, inspecting their troops or visiting their cities, his influence was ever at work, to temper the mortifications of surrender, by raising the ideal of an united Fatherland, and by his personal charm and genial manner to reveal to them in the representative of Prussia a friend, and not a conqueror. As his heart naturally went out to all men, and as he had a real and strong affection for all Germans, to whatever state they belonged, the part he had to play was a very welcome one. Moreover, as he had entered the campaign with a heavy heart, though fully convinced of its necessity, he never ceased subsequently to do all that was in his power to restore the natural bond between Austrians and Prussians, and remove the traces of their temporary estrangement.

Notwithstanding the ominous development of the Luxembourg question, and the tension with France, which never wholly subsided after the Treaty of Prague, the next few years were spent in peace, and the Crown Prince resumed his command of the Second Army Corps. At the end of 1866 he was once more in Russia, for the marriage of the Tsarevitch, Grand Duke Alexander, and in the following year he visited the Paris Exhibition with the Crown Princess. While they were there King William also arrived, and for a while it seemed as if these visits had succeeded in dispelling somewhat the feeling of mistrust between the neighbour nations. In 1868 the Crown Prince went to Turin, to be present at the marriage of Prince Humbert. The latter had been in Berlin the previous year, and with this visit renewed the acquaintance the two Princes had formed in Milan some years previously, and strengthened that cordial friendship between the future rulers of Germany and Italy which continued unbroken to the last. Their positions were not altogether dissimilar. The making of Italy was as yet only partially accomplished, but the campaign of 1866 had greatly lightened the task of King Victor Emmanuel and Cavour. In every Italian city which was visited by the Crown Prince enthusiastic demonstrations testified how sensible the populations were to the debt they owed to Germany. The martial bearing and the winning manner of the hero of

Sadowa appealed directly to the warm temperament of the Italian people, who gave him a Southern welcome, and it was a source of unmixed pleasure to the Royal traveller to find that lie had won the love of a people whose land he loved so well. Among the many personal friends of the Crown Prince in Italy may be mentioned the celebrated Statesmen, Marco Minghetti, Giovanni Morelli, and Count Robilant.

In the same year, the Wedding day of Queen Victoria and Prince Albert, and the anniversary of the Princess Royal's christening, was marked by another conspicuous event in the family of the Crown Prince. A fourth son was born, who seemed sent to fill the sad gap which the death of his little brother had made two years before. Alexander, the present Emperor of Russia, was sponsor to Prince Waldemar, and the christening took place on King William's seventy-first birthday, at Berlin. He was a child of unusual promise, who inherited all the brightness of his father's nature, with that physical beauty which is so often the privilege of those whom the gods love. His little life was long enough to win the hearts of all who were brought near him, and his early death, in his eleventh year, left a gap which could never be filled. It was by the side of this much-loved child that the father chose his last resting-place, when the great tragedy which the passing year has witnessed drew to its close.

In November, 1869, the Sovereigns of all the Maritime Powers were invited to take part in the ceremonious opening of the Suez Canal; and this invitation afforded the Crown Prince, who was deputed to represent the King, an opportunity of realizing the long-cherished plan of a journey through the East. Pausing on his way to make a pilgrimage to

Dante's grave at Ravenna, he crossed from Brindisi by Corfu to Corinth. From Athens he sailed to Constantinople, where the Sultan made over to his guest the concession of an ancient monastery of the Knights of St. John in Jerusalem, which was to furnish the site for a German Protestant Church and hospital. Embarking thence, he arrived on the 3rd of November at Jaffa, and, escorted by a detachment of Marines from the Hertha, started at once for the Holy City, which was reached on the following day, after a night in camp at Bab-el-Wady. Jerusalem is now no longer the goal of pilgrims from the Catholic countries of Europe; but Greeks and Armenians still make their way in numbers to the Holy Sepulchre, and they were a motley throng of all the peoples of the East that lined the narrow streets to witness the Prince's entry. As ever, full of consideration for all about him, he turned to the Marines in his escort, and bade them keep close to him, that they might not miss any of the sights. The deep impression made by the haunting spirit of a spot so familiar through long and tender association, found record in the following entry in the diary in which he never failed to chronicle his observations and experiences: -

'I shall never, as long as I live, forget that first evening in Jerusalem, when I saw the sunset from the Mount of Olives, and that wondrous peace of Nature supervened which even in any other place has a solemn character of its own. Here the spirit could lift itself over earthly things, and dwell uninterruptedly in those thoughts which move the heart of every Christian when he looks hack on that great work of redemption, which found upon this hallowed spot its loftiest expression. To read over again one's favourite passages in the Gospels at such a place is in itself an act of worship.'

From Jerusalem, Bethlehem and the graves of the Patriarchs were visited, and after a brief excursion to Lebanon and Damascus the Crown Prince re-embarked for Port Said. The ceremonies connected with the opening of the Suez Canal were over in time to enable him to reach the first cataract of the Nile, and even to penetrate some distance into Nubia, before rejoining the Crown Princess and his family for the Christmas rejoicing at Cannes, where they had been staying with Princess Alice, whose husband had accompanied the Crown Prince on his travels. The last days of the year were spent at Paris, where the Emperor Napoleon paid them a visit at their hotel. They were 'struck by finding him changed and ailing and much dejected.' In the course of conversation the Emperor mentioned that he had appointed a new Minister, M. Ollivier. Thence, on the morning of the New Year, little anticipating what eventful days it was to bring him, the Crown Prince returned to Berlin. Before that year was over he met the Emperor Napoleon once again - the morning after the capitulation of Sedan.

William I, King of Prussia and German Emperor

V.

1870 — 1871.

THE Spring and early Summer of 1870 had passed uneventfully; the Crown Prince had been sent by his doctors for a cure to Carlsbad, from which he returned in April; and the only event which had marked the year with importance in his family was the birth of a daughter. Princess Sophie, on the 14th of June. The King had gone to Ems, as was his annual habit, when suddenly the crisis came, and the war which had so long been anticipated took Europe by surprise. This is not a place to enter into the causes, immediate or remote, which led to the eventful struggle, nor is any detailed description contemplated of that memorable campaign. So much only will be dealt with in the following pages as may serve to throw light upon the military genius and character of the subject of the present sketch.

After his well-known interview with M. Benedetti, the King returned immediately to Berlin. He was met at Brandenburg by the Crown Prince. Both appreciated the full gravity of the moment and the issues that were at stake; for now, if ever, the question of an united Germany was to be finally decided, and

Prussia was to triumph or to disappear. All along the route two private secretaries had been constantly occupied in deciphering the telegraphic messages which were handed in at every station; and it was on the King's arrival at Berlin that the Crown Prince read to him, by the flickering light of a gas-jet in the station waiting-room, a despatch from Paris announcing the stormy meeting in the French chambers, which clearly indicated the condition of the public mind in Paris. It was to be war; and the King on learning its contents simply said: ' I think I can only answer this message by ordering the mobilization of the whole German army, and in half an hour I shall be ready to sign the necessary papers.' The gas lamp by which the eventful message was read was afterwards taken from its place and retained as a cherished relic.

The plan of campaign had long been prepared, and all went forward with order and precision. On the 19th of July the French Chargé d'Affaires at Berlin handed in the declaration of war, and the whole fighting strength of Germany was already mobilizing and streaming to the Rhine. The King assumed the supreme command of the united German Army, while General Moltke, as Chief of the Staff, accompanied his headquarters, and directed the military operations. The available forces were divided into three armies. The first, commanded by General von Steinmitz, was ordered to concentrate on the Moselle, in the neighbourhood of Treves. The second was placed under the command of Prince Frederick Charles, whose headquarters were first fixed at Mayence, and directed to press forward to the frontier. The Third Army, which was to concentrate on the Upper Rhine, and to form the left, or southern wing, was similarly to advance across the frontier, keeping up close communication with the centre. It was commanded by the Crown Prince. His Chief of the Staff was General von Blumenthal; the Artillery were under the orders of Lieutenant-General Herekt, and the Engineers under Major-General Schulz. The Crown Prince was well fitted, both by his character and his rank, to assume the difficult task of leading and conciliating the various elements of which the Third Army was composed. At least a dozen different dialects of German were spoken in its ranks. It consisted of the two Bavarian Army Corps, the combined Corps of Baden and Württemberg, and the Fifth, Sixth, and Eleventh Prussian Army Corps, with the Second and Fourth Cavalry divisions, amongst which might be found Westphalians, Hessians, and Thuringians, with the regiments from Waldeck and Frankfort.

On the 24th of July, the christening of Princess Sophie took place. It was an anxious party that met round the baptismal font, for there were few present there who were not under orders for the front. The gentlemen were already in their high boots and campaigning accoutrements. Emotion, anxiety, and excitement made the King unable to hold his little granddaughter at the baptismal font, according to wont, and he deputed the task to the Queen Augusta. On the 25th, the Crown Prince once more went to church, and received the Communion with the Princess, and early on the morning of the 26th he departed without taking leave; he wished to spare his wife the agony of parting. He first proceeded to Munich, to pay a hasty visit to King Ludwig of Bavaria. The reception accorded him wherever he showed himself, the enthusiasm which greeted his appearance by the side of the young King in the theatre, augured well for the spirit of the Bavarian troops. Proceeding from Munich to Stuttgart, he paused on his way at Ingoldstadt to introduce himself as their commander to the assembled officers of the Bavarian Army, and addressed them in the following words: 'I cannot sufficiently express to you the honour which I feel has been done me by your King in entrusting his army to my command. Let us not conceal from ourselves that we have before us a momentous struggle, but the universal enthusiasm which we are witnesses of from every corner of Germany bids me hope that, with God's help, it will be a victorious struggle, which will lead at last to a peace that shall crown our German Fatherland with prosperity. Let us then rely on our good cause, upon our good sword! ' By Stuttgart and Carlsruhe he proceeded to Spires, where his headquarters were first established, and at once began that difficult task, which it is his special merit to have carried through so successfully, of consolidating his army, morally as well as practically, and welding its many elements into one harmonious whole. On the day of his arrival, the 30th, he was in the camp of the Bavarians, observing, encouraging, asking a friendly question of this man and that, and spreading by his genial presence, that contagious enthusiasm which is worth so much on the eve of battle. The same day he issued his Proclamation to the Army: -

'SOLDIERS OF THE THIRD ARMY,

'Appointed by my royal father Commander-in-Chief of the Third Army, I greet the troops of Prussia, Bavaria, Württemberg, and Baden, who are henceforth under my command. It fills me with pride and satisfaction to be advancing' against the foe at the head of an army composed of men from every part of our common German Fatherland, for the national cause, for the right, for the honour of Germany. We are marching to a great and grave struggle, but convinced of the justice of our cause, and relying on your bravery, your endurance, and your manliness, we have no misgivings as to its victorious issue. Therefore let us hold fast to our true brotherhood in arms, that with God's help we may unroll our banners to new victories for the glory and the peace of our united Fatherland.

'FREDERICK WILLIAM,
'Crown Prince of Prussia.'

On the 3rd of August the Prince pushed on his headquarters to Landau, and issued orders that on the following day his troops should cross the Lauter, and enter hostile territory. Reconnaissances had proved that the French showed no disposition to strike the first blow, and the fact that the frontier lines were still unoccupied, justified the presumption that they were not yet fully prepared. The Seventh French Corps d'Armée, under General Felix Douay, detailed to protect the Southern passes of the Vosges, which was the first to come to close quarters with the Third Army, had been the last to complete its mobilization, and the General was quite unprepared to carry out an instruction despatched on the 27th of July to join the division of Marshal MacMahon, whose troops were concentrated near Strasburg. The strategic plan of the Emperor Napoleon to unite the armies of Metz and Strasburg, to cross the Rhine with an overwhelming force and occupy Baden and the Palatinate, was anticipated by the rapidity of the German mobilization and advance.

As day broke on the morning of the 4th the Crown Prince advanced on Weissenburg. The town itself, situated on the river Lauter, was fortified with obsolete ramparts dating from the last century, but the heights to the south-west, known as the Geisberg, afforded a very strong position, and were occupied by General Douay with eleven battalions of infantry and four batteries of artillery. The Crown Prince arrived on the field of battle at a quarter past nine, and directed operations in person. Before midday the town was in the hands of the Germans, and what remained of the garrison their prisoners. The whole attack was then concentrated on the Geisberg. Many of the regiments had been as much as eight hours on the march, hut their determined advance carried all before it, and the French, who were heavily outnumbered, abandoned their positions one by one. A stubborn resistance was made in the Schloss, with its outhouses, crowning the summit, and a first attempt to carry the position by storm was repulsed; but still new troops succeeded. The French, with great coolness, reserved their fire till the enemy was within certain range, and then opened a deadly hail from every point of vantage. The colours of the Seventh Royal Grenadiers, who led the advancing column, were passed from hand to hand, as one by one the bearers were shot down. At length a battery was brought to bear upon the stronghold, now surrounded on every side by the Prussian and Bavarian troops, and towards one o'clock the survivors surrendered, and the first battle of the war was won.

The victorious regiments were drawn up on the heights as the Crown Prince rode up the bloody slopes of the Geisberg, where the dead and wounded were lying on every side, in evidence of the severity of the struggle. On his way he paused here and there to speak to a wounded soldier, and then standing still in the midst of his young troops, still black with powder-smoke and soiled with the dust of battle, he addressed a few stirring words of gratitude to each and all for their steadiness and gallantry. The tattered flag of the Royal Grenadiers was brought him, and he kissed it, and embraced the wounded commander of the regiment, Major von Kaisenberg, who had fallen at the head of the storming column, with the colours in his hand. Then, learning that General Douay had fallen in the battle, he desired to be shown the body of this distinguished officer. The Crown Prince went in alone to the peasant's cottage where he lay; it was a moving and suggestive sigh; in the morning their chances were equal; in the flush of victory, the pathetic contrast of this brave man's fate now touched him deeply; not a soul of all the thousands he had commanded was watching at his side, only his dog sat whining by the corpse.

The German troops had undoubtedly outnumbered the French considerably. Some sixteen battalions had been engaged on their side, while the division of General Douay numbered less than 9,000 men; but the strength of the French position had more than compensated for the inequality of numbers, and the steadiness and determination shown by the Germans had been exemplary. Besides, the first ordeal had been successfully overcome; Prussians and Bavarians had conquered side by side. The importance of the victory could scarcely be over-estimated, but it was dearly bought, for ninety-one officers and upwards of 1,400 men were left on the battlefield.

In the afternoon of the 4th headquarters were advanced to Schweighofen, and on the following day to Sulz, some seven miles from the village of Wörth.

The news of the defeat of his advance-guard reached Marshal MacMahon the same evening at Strasburg. He at once pushed forward with all the forces he could muster, to retrieve, if possible, the disaster, by covering the passes of the Vosges, and attempting to drive the invading army back over the Alsatian frontier. With this object he took up a strong position, on the 5th, along a line of wooded heights to the west of the village of Wörth, in communication with the more distant fortress of Bitsch. In the rear of his position lay Reichshofen, connected with Wörth by a high road; to the north-east was the village of Froschweiler, to the south Elsasshausen, the left and right centres of the French lines, the extreme right extending as far as Mörsbrunn, and the extreme left to Neuweiler, in the direction of Bitsch. The attack was expected on the 7tli, and it had been the intention of the Commander of the Third Army to postpone the decisive encounter till that day, when he would have been able to bring all his five army corps into action simultaneously; but during the night of the 5th, and in the early morning of the 6th, a lively interchange of shots took place between the French outposts and the advance guard of the Fifth Prussian Corps in the centre, and the Second Bavarian Corps on the right. The General in command of the Fifth Corps, noticing considerable movement in the French lines about 4 a.m., was under the impression that they were about to retreat from their positions, and ordered a reconnaissance in force. From this reconnaissance the decisive battle developed itself; for though orders were despatched to the various commanders to avoid bringing on a general action at present, matters had already gone too far to make this course practicable, and the French had assumed the offensive. The commander of the Eleventh Corps, which formed the left of the first line, seeing the Fifth

Corps and the Bavarians engaged, prepared to render assistance, and by midday all three corps were fully employed. At half-past twelve, the Crown Prince and his Staff arrived on the field of battle, and about the same time the First Bavarian Corps and the Württemberg division, which had had upwards of ten miles to march that morning, were drawing into line, while the Baden regiments were following hard behind.

The first object of the Crown Prince was to drive the French out of Worth, and having done this, to move forward and contest the positions held by the left wing of Marshal MacMahon's army, extending in a north-easterly direction to Froschweiler, while a simultaneous movement was to be directed against the French right at Elsasshausen, to prevent the possibility of their attacking the Fifth Prussian Corps in flank.

Immediately after the arrival of the Commander-in-Chief, an advance was ordered along the whole line. After a brief but severe struggle, Wörth was carried by General von Kirchback, and two attempts to retake it were repulsed. Meanwhile the Eleventh Corps, advancing against the French right, drove them back from Mörsbrunn to Elsasshausen, and joined hands with the centre, now moving upon Froschweiler. All along the road from Mörsbrunn they had fought a desperate hand to hand struggle, through woods and vineyards; the ground did not permit of reforming, and the fight was man for man. The dead and wounded lay clubbed or bayonetted, French and German, side by side or locked together in the death-grapple where they fell. Just outside Elsasshausen General von Bose, who commanded the corps, was severely wounded, but still managed to keep his seat in the saddle; an hour later he received a second wound at Froschweiler. Thus the French right, still fighting with unremitted courage, was forced to yield step by step along the whole position, and the progress of the German left was the signal for a concentrated attack on Froschweiler. About three o'clock in the afternoon the batteries opened fire upon it from three sides, and as the flames of the burning houses marked the havoc which the shells had made, the combined right and centre advanced to storm the heights. The Crown Prince, when he had issued his final orders, leapt upon his horse and rode after the storming columns, through Wörth and across the field of battle. At four o'clock Marshal MacMahon recognized that his position was no longer tenable, and gave orders to retire. It was at this point, in order to cover his retreat on Reichshofen, and stay the pursuit of the victorious Germans left from Elsasshausen, that he ordered that desperate charge of the brigade of Cuirassiers, which, executed with the unfaltering devotion of a forlorn hope, became one of the most tragic and heroic episodes in a story abounding in tragedy and heroism. If the roads beyond Reichshofen to Bitsch, Zabern, and Strasburg were secured, it was at a frightful cost. The French cavalry charged into a valley of death; mown down by the simultaneous fire of artillery and infantry, they lay in ordered ranks, with their faces to the foe that few of them ever reached, a grisly army of the dead.

The French had fought with the utmost gallantry, and all that mortal men could do to avert disaster had been done; but attacked simultaneously on the North, East, and South, with his retreat threatened, the Marshal had no choice but to retire. He reached Zabern on the following day, and withdrew thence to Chalons, while other portions of the army fell back on

Bitsch and Strasburg. In the evening the Crown Prince rode over the battlefield and congratulated his troops on this decisive victory; the massed bands were playing the national hymn as he rode up the heights of Froschweiler, greeted by the joyful cheers of officers and men. But it was a scene of desolation that met his eyes, the dead of Reichshofen lay in grim and ghastly heaps, and there were terrible gaps in his own regiments. On the French side some 200 officers and 9,000 men were prisoners, while the losses in killed and wounded amounted to upwards of 6,000, but the victory was obtained at the cost of 500 officers and more than 10,000 men *hors de combat*. Amongst the distinguished French officers who had been wounded, the Crown Prince found General Raoult, who succumbed to his injuries a few weeks later, lying on his camp-bed, and, grasping his hand, spoke a few words of kindly solicitude, and while offering to convey any communication he might wish to his family, desired him to command his services.

The following day, the 7th, was devoted to rest. In the morning the Crown Prince again rode over the field of battle, and was then for the first time able to appreciate the full measure of the carnage and desolation that the day's work had made. In the garden of a farm-house which had not suffered from the passing storm, he found a Bavarian trooper, who had made himself very much at home, enjoying a quiet breakfast, and as was his wont addressed a few friendly words to him. Standing at attention with his hand at the salute, the honest Bavarian allowed his enthusiasm to carry him away, and exclaimed: 'If only we had had your Royal Highness to lead us in 1866, you would have seen how we would have thrashed those cursed Prussians!' - 'I never,' said the Crown Prince, 'received a compliment that pleased me better.'

The road now lay open into the heart of France, and the advance was continued through the passes of the Yosges. The Baden contingent was told off to invest the fortress of Strasburg, and on the 11th, from headquarters at Petersbach, the following proclamation was issued to the victorious troops: -

'SOLDIERS OF THE THIRD ARMY,

'Having with the victorious battle of Weissenburg crossed the frontier into French territory, and then by the brilliant victory of Wörth driven the French out of Alsace, we have by now advanced across the Yosges far into France, and have established communications with the First and Second Armies, before whose successful arms the foe has equally been compelled to retire.[1] It is your great gallantry, your high spirit, your endurance under every difficulty and exertion, that we have to thank for these important achievements. In the name of the King of Prussia, our Commander-in-Chief, and in the name of the Allied Princes, I thank you, and I am proud to find myself at the head of an army against which the enemy has hitherto been unable to hold his ground, whose deeds our common German Fatherland is watching with enthusiasm — FREDERICK WILLIAM.'

Simple words and unadorned, but words which went home to every man among them, who knew that appeal to their common nationality was no empty phrase with their leader, whom they would have followed, Bavarians, Württembergers, and all of them, to the end of the world. For by now their confidence in him was equal to their regard, and each individual felt himself to be the object of his leader's forethought and solicitude. 'In the hospitals,' says one of his biographers, 'the wounded seem to forget their pain when he drew near, and many in their delirium could speak of nothing but their leader.' And how he had won the hearts of his army the following extract from the letter of a Bavarian officer will serve to illustrate: -

'It is the Crown Prince, in the first place, that we have to thank for the brotherly relations which subsist between the troops, for Prussians and Bavarians going arm-in-arm. Even the private soldiers are made his comrades for life and death: he speaks to them, not condescendingly', but with such an unmistakable ring of personal interest, and with such a genial manner, that the fellows' hearts go out to him every time. And so does his to them. So overcome was he the other day in conferring an exceptional military distinction on a private soldier, that in his enthusiasm he placed his hands upon the hero's shoulders and kissed him. There was a moment's breathless silence, and the muskets trembled in the soldiers' hands.'

On the 16th of August the Crown Prince arrived with his Staff at Nancy, and awaited news of the movements of the First and Second Armies. On the 19th two officers who had been despatched to the King's headquarters at Pont-à-Mousson returned with news of the three battles that had been fought round Metz, of the last of which, Gravelotte, they had themselves been eye-witnesses. The army of Marshal Bazaine was now shut up in Metz, and surrounded by seven army corps under the command of Prince Frederick Charles, it was precluded from taking any further active part in the campaign. On the 20th the Crown Prince went to Pont-à-Mousson, and saw the King for the first time after an eventful month. The coveted distinction of the Iron Cross of the first class was here bestowed upon him, but with his distinctive chivalry he declared he could not wear it unless a similar decoration were bestowed on General von Blumenthal.

Meanwhile the enemy was straining every nerve to form a new army at Chalons, where the broken columns of MacMahon's force had halted in their retreat. These were reinforced by the corps of General Failly and two divisions from Belfort, while large numbers of the Garde Mobile were despatched in haste from Paris. The position was well selected, but no preparations had been made for the reception of such a number of troops, and it became untenable before the rapid advance of the Germans. The day after the battle of Gravelotte a council of war had been held at the German headquarters, at which it had been decided to form a Fourth Army (the Army of the Meuse) composed of three corps drawn off from the Second Army, to be placed under the command of the Crown Prince of Saxony. This army was to co-operate with the Third Army, and their first object was to be the destruction of the force now mustering at Chalons. On the night of the 20th, the Crown Prince rejoined his Staff at Yaucouleurs, to which the headquarters had been moved from Nancy. In illustration of the spirit in which he carried out the instructions of his King and Father to wage no war on the peaceful inhabitants of France, the following proclamation, issued to the inhabitants of Nancy, will be read with interest: -

'Germany is at war with the Emperor of the French, not with the French people. The population need fear no hostile measures. I am occupied in restoring the people, and especially for the town of

Nancy, the means of communication which were broken by the French Army I trust that business and trade will revive, and that the authorities will remain at their posts. I claim for the maintenance of my army only the excess of provision which is not required for the support of the native population. All that are peacefully inclined, and particularly the population of the town of Nancy, may count upon the most indulgent treatment.'

And this was literally carried out. The military field-post was made available for the inhabitants of Nancy, and with extraordinary rapidity the telegraph wires and railway lines which the French troops had destroyed were set in working order again.

The fortress of Toul, which lay on the line of march, offered a determined resistance. The Crown Prince had ordered that the town was to be spared as much as the exigencies of war would permit, and especially that the Cathedral, a masterpiece of Gothic architecture, was to be kept well out of the line of fire. Bombarded for a whole day, Toul still held out, and the troops investing the fortress were ordered to rejoin the main body marching on Chalons, a detachment being left behind to mask it until the reserves came up, when the surrender was to be enforced. On the 23rd headquarters were at Ligny. The King had left Pont-à-Mousson that morning, and after passing the night at Commercy, was timed to arrive at Ligny towards noon on the 24th. The streets of the little town were bright with uniforms, and all its inhabitants had crowded out to see the young commander of the Third Army, who, surrounded by his Staff, was awaiting the King's arrival. As the clock struck twelve a Hussar came galloping across the market-place and delivered a sealed order to the Prince, who hastily read its contents, and passed it on to General Blumenthal. There was great news. The French had evacuated Chalons on the 21st, and the town was already occupied by the German cavalry. The King arrived soon after one o'clock at Ligny, and the changed aspect of affairs was considered. The direction northwards taken by Marshal MacMahon's Army afforded strong grounds for the presumption that it was the Emperor's intention, if possible, to relieve Bazaine, and intercepted despatches subsequently confirmed the accuracy of this surmise. His first plan, to retire on Paris with the army of Chalons, was abandoned in deference to reports from the capital, where the Empress Eugenie warned him that to abandon Bazaine and to return himself to Paris would be the signal for revolution.

In the King's headquarters at Bar-le-Duc a council of war was held. The determination to despatch the Fourth Army and the two Bavarian corps only of the Third Army, to intercept Marshal MacMahon's progress, was combated by the Crown Prince, who maintained that it was of paramount importance that all available forces should combine to strike a decisive blow in the North, even if the advance on Paris were delayed. His advice, supported by the weight of General Blumenthal's opinion, prevailed, and consequently the whole of the Third Army, in conjunction with the Fourth, faced round to the right and hurried by forced marches to the North. On the 28th reconnaissances took place which left no further doubt as to the whereabouts of Marshal MacMahon's Army. After a series of engagements in which the Crown Prince of Saxony carried off the palm at Beaumont, the French drew back on the fortress of Sedan, which, on the evening of the 31st August, was surrounded on three sides by the German troops.

It would be out of the question here, in the short space which can be accorded to it, to give any account of the memorable battle which dealt the French Empire its death-blow. Fighting began at daybreak; Marshal MacMahon had drawn up his army in a semi-circle round Sedan, extending from the north by east to south; the west was undefended, and passage over the Meuse at Donchéry was thus open to the German advance. The task before the Third and Fourth Armies, which the two Crown Princes led, under the supreme command of the King himself, was to surround the French position, preventing the possibility of an eastward move, and at the same time cutting off their retreat across the Belgian frontier to the north, while, to meet the eventuality of a westward movement, should the three sides of their front be driven back, the Sixth Army Corps had been detached to take up a strong- position some twenty miles to the west of Sedan, with instructions to hold the roads and passes till the main body had time to come up. By four o'clock in the afternoon the French positions were all in the hands of the Germans, and a living wall, consisting of eight Army Corps, surrounded the whole French army in the fortress of Sedan. A brief pause ensued; only to the north the cannon thundered, and in the village of Bazeilles a desperate fight still raged in the ruined streets. Then, as no message of surrender came, the guns began to play on the devoted fortress, great clouds of smoke rolled up, and forked flames began to issue from the burning houses.

Colonel von Bronsart, who was despatched by the King to demand the surrender, found a white flag raised upon the walls, and was admitted within the gates. He had asked to be led to the General in command, and was conducted to a room in the Prefecture, where he found himself face to face with the Emperor Napoleon. From him the Emperor learned that the King of Prussia was present with the besieging army, and despatched General Reille in company with Colonel von Bronsart to deliver to his Majesty the celebrated letter, in which he wrote that, having failed to find death in the midst of his troops, there was nothing left him but to surrender his sword. Shortly before their arrival the King and the Crown Prince had met. It was now seven o'clock. We are all familiar with that twilight picture; the veteran King standing on a slight eminence, close behind him the Crown Prince, Bismarck, Moltke, Blumenthal; General Reille advancing towards them with bare head, and the fateful letter in his hand. Three years before General Reille had been in attendance on the Crown Prince during his visit to the French Exhibition. The latter recognizes him, and immediately steps forward to greet him. The King reads the letter, and passes it to the Princes who are with him, and to his Staff, then he turns to the Crown Prince and clasps him to his heart. It had not been known from the first that the Emperor was himself in Sedan; with his surrender there was at least a hope that the war which had already entailed such heavy sacrifices was at an end.

But the end was not yet to be. MacMahon's army were all prisoners of war, the army of Bazaine was interned at Metz; but the events of the 4th of September in Paris decided an advance on the capital. On the 6th, the King and Crown Prince arrived in Rheims, and a few days were devoted to rest. The people of Rheims were astonished to see the Commander of the Third Army, accompanied only by one or two of his Staff, quietly walking through the streets of their city, and studying the marvels of their famous Cathedral. Every measure of indulgence was accorded to the population during the German occupation; an order from headquarters gave instructions that no troops were to be quartered on the poorer inhabitants, and the local newspapers bore witness to the courtesy and moderation of their invaders. During his stay at Rheims, the Crown Prince addressed an appeal to all the States of Germany to join in founding an institution similar to that which he had inaugurated in 1864 for the relief of the victims of war. 'As this war,' he wrote, 'has called out an united German Army, in which the sons of every race are contending in brotherly rivalry for the palm of valour, so let the provision for the invalided and the destitute whom war will leave on our hands be an undertaking which the whole German race shall co-operate in.'

Meanwhile, at home in Germany, the women's work was no less zealous than that of their sons and husbands at the front. The Queen and the Crown Princess were incessantly at work, organizing help for the destitute at home, and relief for the wounded and the prisoners. Near the French frontier almost every house had been turned into a hospital. The Crown Princess herself was established at Hamburg, in order to be nearer to the seat of war, and in the great 'Lazareth'[2] here, under her direct superintendence, as many as a thousand beds were at one time made up. The Crown Princess's work was additionally arduous, as she had to pay frequent visits to her sister, Princess Alice, at Darmstadt, whose baby was born in October while her husband was away at the war. Yet hardly a day passed without her attendance, not a patient lay there who did not receive some kindly word of sympathy, a sympathy that went directly home to

99

each of those who knew that their royal leader had never spared himself in battle, and that there were no less anxious hearts in the old Hamburg Palace than in the humblest cottage that had sent a father or a son to light.

At his headquarters of Coulommiers, on the 15th September, the Crown Prince occupied the house in which King Frederick William III, with his three eldest sons, had rested, during the advance of the Allies to Paris in 1814. On the 19th the soldiers of the Third Army looked down upon the distant spires and domes of Paris, and on the following day the Crown Prince established himself in the Prefecture at Versailles. On the arrival of the King he gave up this residence to his father, and transferred his own headquarters to the villa 'Les Ombrages,' the property of Madame Andrée Walther. And so the long siege began with its repeated sorties and all its well-known incidents. The news of the fall of Metz was received at Versailles on the 28th October, and the King commemorated this event by creating a new precedent in the family of Hohenzollern, in bestowing the baton of Field-Marshal on his son and his nephew, Prince Frederick Charles. At the close of the rescript in which he announced this determination to his son, after commenting on the brilliant achievements of the Third Army, he said: -

'You are, therefore, entitled to the highest grade of military rank, and I hereby appoint you Field-Marshal. It is the first time that this distinction, which I also confer upon Frederick Charles, has been granted to Princes of our house. But the successes gained in this campaign have been of a character, and have led to issues of an importance, entirely without a precedent hitherto, and, therefore, I feel justified in departing from the tradition of our family. What I as a father feel, in being able to express to you my own thanks, and the country's, in such a form as this, it needs no words to describe. Your loving and grateful father, WILLIAM.'

And so Christmas came, the first Christmas from home. The bitter Winter weather had set in with terrible severity; hut there was not wanting the brighter side. The French population of Versailles had found a friend in their enemy, a friend whose ears were always open to listen to an honest grief, who had guaranteed their town and its treasures his royal protection, and who did all that lay in his power to alleviate the horrors of war, so that even here the 'Notre Fritz' was fast becoming a household word. When the guns of Mont Valérien opened fire on St. Cloud, it was the German troops under his command who saved all that was saved from the treasures of the Palace, the removable works of art and the library; and, on the appeal of M. Régnault, the distinguished scientist, he organized a little expedition to save all that was irreplaceable, the models, the drawings, and the moulds, from the China factory of Sèvres, which was also in danger of destruction from the French fires. *'Fas est et ab hoste doceri.'* The subjoined letter, from his hostess in Versailles to a friend, which has recently been published in Germany, speaks for itself:

'Those were indeed bad times, but we thought ourselves happy to be under the protection of that stately and friendly gentleman, who appears to us, as we now think of him, to have been a good genius who warded off mischief from our household. Although, according to the laws of war, he was our master, and the owner for the time of all that we had, he behaved himself always as if he were our guest. I can never forget the gentleness with which he used to ask for anything, whether for himself or his Adjutant, apologizing for giving us trouble, fearful of causing any inconvenience, and enquiring whether this or that would interfere with our own arrangements. On Christmas Eve, when a huge chest arrived from Berlin for the Crown Prince, he invited his hostess and her family to partake of his Christmas cake. 'This cake,' said he, as he cut off slices for the French ladies, 'was baked by my wife, and you must oblige me to taste it.' He then chatted to them about the Christmas festival in his own happy household, and translated passages from the letter of the Crown Princess and the letters of his two eldest children. 'In those fateful days,' she continues, 'we learned to know the whole good and open heart of our late Emperor. On the terrible 19th of January, 1871, when there was fighting at Mount Yalerien, Bougival, and St. Cloud, and our troops were driven back upon Paris, many thousands of my fellow-countrymen were taken prisoners. At six o'clock in the evening the Crown Prince had learned that among them there were several men who were not professional soldiers - lawyers, artists, teachers, merchants, and others. He asked the French officers who were taken prisoners to notify to these civilians that if they gave their names to him he would place escorts at their service, so that they might return to their homes and work. This generous noblesse in your Prince made a deep impression upon the French mind. It has never been forgotten, and I know with what profound respect the knightly conqueror was spoken of at the time. The older folk in France, in whom the recollection of those days must always abide, hold the memory of the noble Emperor Friedrich in the greatest esteem.'

Just after Christmas the heavy siege guns, which

had at length arrived, opened fire on the city and its surrounding forts. The Crown Prince himself was at first against the bombardment, but the terrible losses of the German troops in the bloody battle before Paris, and the unprecedented severity of the Winter, made it imperative that the protracted siege should be terminated as soon as possible.

Meanwhile the long-desired consummation of the German idea was drawing near. After the battle of Sedan, the South German States had signified their readiness to adhere to the Northern Confederation; before Christmas all preliminaries were complete, and the Princes, on the proposition of King Ludwig of Bavaria, joined with the Northern Diet in inviting King William to assume the Imperial Dignity over an united Germany. The 18th of January, 1871, was fixed for the solemnization of this great event, and the Crown Prince was entrusted with all the preparations for the ceremony. Every regiment in the army of investment was instructed to send its colours in charge of an officer and two non-commissioned officers to Versailles, and all the higher officers who could be spared from duty were ordered to attend, for the army was to represent the German nation at this memorable scene. The Crown Prince escorted his father from the Prefecture to the palace of Versailles, where all the German Princes or their representatives were assembled in the Galerie des Glaces. A special service was read by the military chaplains, and then the Emperor, mounting on the dais, announced his assumption of Imperial authority, and instructed his Chancellor to read the Proclamation issued to the whole German nation. Then the Crown Prince, as the first subject of the Empire, came forward, and performed the solemn act of homage, kneeling down before his Imperial Father. The Emperor raised him and clasped to his arms the son who had toiled and fought and borne so great a share in achieving what many generations had desired in vain, and fulfilling the prophetic words of King Frederick William IV: 'An imperial crown must be won upon the field of battle.'

The following day the last desperate sortie from the beleaguered city took place. The battle was in the immediate vicinity of Versailles, and the Crown Prince was on the field throughout the day. The French fought with the courage of despair, for the city was exhausted, and unless they could dislodge the Germans from their positions and break through, surrender was inevitable. But when the early darkness closed, this final effort had not availed, and four days afterwards the first overtures were made for a cessation of hostilities.

On the 7th of March the Crown Prince left Versailles. The war was over, and on the last Sunday, as he sat at service in the little church, which he had never failed to attend during his long residence there, the words of the text, 'How beautiful upon the mountains are the feet of him that bringeth good tidings, that publisheth peace,' must have fallen upon his ears with a peculiar sweetness and a deeper meaning than ever before. After a brief journey to Rouen and Amiens, to inspect the Army of the North, and convey the Emperor's thanks to General von Goeben for his decisive victory at St. Quentin, he rejoined his Imperial Father at Nancy, where he issued his last address to his army. 'I take my leave of you,' it concluded, 'Prussian and Bavarian corps, soldiers of Württemberg and Baden, with the hope and in full confidence that the brotherhood of arms and the spirit of union cemented on the bloody field of battle may never disappear, but increase in vitality and strength, to the honour, the glory, and the blessing of our common Fatherland.' But the parting was not to be a final one, for, needless to say, he was at Munich in July, when the Bavarian troops returned to make their triumphal entry. It was a touching meeting, and the words which he spoke at the ensuing banquet were a message to every man who had fought under his command, which he might bear back with pride to his mountain village, and repeat in time to come with all those memories and episodes which many a cottage home throughout the length and breadth of Germany still teems with. 'In this campaign,' he said, 'I learned what we may expect from Bavaria in good and evil days. With the help of the Bavarians we have won an honourable peace, which we hope will endure. And as in war they did their duty, so may they now emulate the rest of the German family in furthering the arts of peace, and in practising in peace the virtues of a soldier.'

After the war of 1870, it became the Crown Prince's annual duty to inspect the military contingents of the South German States, and the associations of the great campaign were thus continually refreshed. It was ever his aim to bind faster those bonds of union which his personal influence had done so much to promote, and, by guaranteeing to the various component elements of the Empire respect for their individual character and institutions, to enlist the public sympathy for the changed order of things.

From Nancy it was one long triumphal progress home. Berlin was reached on the 17th of March; and, though no official reception was allowed, the Royal carriage in which the King and the Crown Prince were to be seen side by side could only proceed at a foot pace through the dense masses that crowded the streets, cheering them with the cheers of a triumphant nation. With one pretty picture the record of the great campaign may fitly close, when, a little later, in response to the call of the people who thronged about his Berlin Palace, a window opened, and they saw in the midst of his young family, and beside the Crown Princess, the hero of so many victories, happy in his own home, with his youngest child in his arms.

Men have judged and will judge his military genius differently. How thorough was his practical knowledge of the soldier's business is clear from the fact that the new drill regulations for the infantry, which by order of the reigning Emperor are to supersede the old ones, had been long planned by him. It was his decisive march at Königgrätz which decided the fate of the day, it was his insistence on the necessity of leading the whole of his Army to Sedan that ensured the surrender of Marshal MacMahon's Army and the person of the Emperor Napoleon. Few great leaders can show such an unvarying record of successes, and none have possessed in a higher degree the most indispensable quality of the successful soldier, the power of attaching to himself the love and confidence of his followers. He showed a rare and striking example of simplicity and unselfishness to his soldiers. He never admitted luxuries, and would not even accept necessaries if he knew that his men were without food and drink. His thought was always for others, never for himself. The verdict of an Englishman, who had the most exceptional opportunities of observing the events which have just been described, cannot fail to be interesting to English readers. General Sir Beauchamp Walker, who in his capacity as British Military Attaché, and no less as a personal friend, accompanied the Crown Prince's Staff throughout the campaigns of 1866 and 1870, writes: -

'The great characteristic which distinguished him was his coolness in difficulty; whatever happened, he and Blumenthal kept their heads clear. His judgment was calm in action, his consideration was humane in success. What more can one say of the noblest man I have ever known!'

*Crown Princess Frederick William and Prince William of
Prussia, 1876*

VI.

1871—1887.

HITHERTO we have followed in the Prince's footsteps, along the path of public duty, and through scenes of continual activity. Now, a long period of peace lies before us, and while considering this quieter picture, we may also glance back again and see how the intervals of rest were spent, and what were the interests and occupations of one who, though circumstances had made him a soldier, was at heart a man of peace. A love of study, an enthusiasm for Art, with a full consciousness of its lofty and ennobling mission, continued with him throughout his life, while he found in the Crown Princess one who shared his cultivated tastes, and actively co-operated in directing those labours of love which it became his especial mission to promote. His own words will best testify what he held the aim of all true Art to be. Speaking at the opening of the Jubilee Exhibition of the Berlin Academy, in 1886, he said: 'But look to it, that our Art be never untrue to its high calling, to be for mankind, high and low, rich and poor, that elevating and spiritualizing influence which helps man up to God. Then, after that, let it fulfil its other calling - the union of nations and individuals, with all their different utterances, in the common worship of the ideal.'

Needless to say, their Court at Berlin was a meeting place for all that was remarkable in various fields of culture. In Berlin and Vienna, of all the European capitals, the distinctions of class are still most rigorously marked, and there is accordingly less social intercourse between the various grades and faculties. Moreover, party spirit still runs very high, opinions coincide with social positions, and the mutual antipathy of the various political denominations is by no means confined to the precincts of the Chamber. The parties at the Crown Prince's Palace, however, formed a bright exception to this somewhat monotonous uniformity of clannishness, and there would be gathered together scholars and theologians, archaeologists and explorers, artists and men of letters, without distinction of birth or political opinion. Many a young and unknown singer, and many a struggling musician, have owed their first introduction to the public notice to the Winter concerts at their palace, and all that was new in the field of design, all that was original or remarkable in Art, was assured beforehand of their interest and support. Our own countrymen can bear witness to the fact that no English author or painter of eminence whom business or pleasure took to Berlin, ever failed to find a warm welcome there; and it was always matter for regret if any such passed through the capital unnoticed or unknown.

It was therefore a peculiar satisfaction to the Crown Prince, debarred as he was by the rule he had made himself, from any participation in affairs of State, when the office of Protector of Public Museums was conferred upon him. Those who have seen them before his interest and energies were enlisted in their behalf, and since, have testified to the extraordinary development and improvement of these collections under his sympathetic control. The Old Museum, founded but little more than fifty years ago, has few rivals in Europe in completeness, certainly none in arrangement. The pictures, judiciously added to by recent purchases, for the most part from England, though still comparatively few in number, are thoroughly representative of the various schools in their rise and evolution; - the print room, enriched under the Prince's regime by the famous acquisitions from the Hamilton Collection, is probably the best managed institution of its kind that exists; - the marbles from Pergamos, recovered by the indomitable perseverance of Herr Humann, have under his auspices been added to reinforce the weaker side of the Museum, its classical sculpture; while it can show, what we in England, with all our wealth of treasures, have not yet been able to afford ourselves, a gallery of casts from the great sculptures of the world, which it was his aim to render complete. The Museum of Industrial Art, corresponding to our own Museum at South Kensington, has grown up entirely under the supervision of the Crown Prince and Princess. A third institution, the Ethnological Museum, in which he took the keenest interest, is still in process of arrangement, and though already open, will not be completed for some time to come.[1]

But it was not only the moral and intellectual progress of the people which the Prince and Princess have been ever zealous to promote; the material prosperity was a matter of no less concern. And so well was their devotion to this work understood in Germany that, on the celebration of their silver wedding, the present which the country placed in their hands was a sum £50,000, collected from the

111

highest and the lowest, and in every portion of the Empire, to be distributed as they judged fit, among the various charities with which they were connected. How thoroughly this gift was appreciated appears from their message of thanks: 'We must express our especial satisfaction at the fact, that our silver wedding has been made the occasion of giving to the day on which we made our marriage vow, and founded, with God's help, the happiness of our lives, its fairest consecration, and a significance which our feelings and our aspirations approve, by the inauguration of charitable institutions, and by collections for objects at once noble and of public utility.'

Space would fail to enumerate all the foundations and institutions which owe their existence to the initiative of the loyal pair, or in which they have taken an active interest. The so-called 'Workmen's Colonies,' whose object is the reclaiming of tramps and finding temporary occupation for the unemployed; the 'Fortbildung's Schule' institutions for the technical and practical education of working-men in their leisure hours, owe much to the Crown Prince's promotion and patronage; while it needs but to mention the Society for the Promotion of Health in the Home, the Victoria School for the Training of Nurses, the Victoria Foundation for the Training of Young Girls in Domestic and Industrial Work, to show the practical nature of the public services to which they devoted themselves with the cordial co-operation of the municipal officers of Berlin. Broad and tolerant in religious opinion, the Crown Prince was a determined opponent of the anti-Semitic movement, and a firm supporter of the liberty of conscience. He was a zealous protector of the order of Freemasons, and a number of speeches made hy him to various lodges are on record, in which the same

112

keynote is always struck, the practical work they have to do, and the necessity of obsolete customs and traditions yielding to the law of human progress.

But it was especially at Potsdam, in the Summer months, away from the restraints of the capital and the absorbing calls of social and public duties, that the home-life of the Soldier-Prince displayed its brightest side. The occupations afforded by the little farm at Bornstedt, the visits to the schools, the care of poorer and humbler neighbours, have been already alluded to. A charming picture was afforded every year, as Christmas came round, when all the tenants of the Bornstedt estate and their children met round the Christmas-tree and the long tables ranged with presents, to distribute which the kindly landlord and his family never failed to come from Berlin. And again, in the Summer, when the school-feast came round, and the playing ground of the little Princes and Princesses was filled with tiny beings, shy and full of awe at first, but before long brimming over with excitement and delight, and carrying away a memory which would never be forgotten of those who led their romps, and stood by to watch their merry games. Indeed, the Crown Prince and Princess were never happier than when they were surrounded by the children of the poor; and every school or institution with which they were in any way connected was sure of its annual invitation.

The education of their own children had from the first absorbed their anxious care. The young Princes were brought up in the strictest simplicity, and early encouraged to take their part in those offices of kindness and charity in which their parents found a pleasurable duty, while by frequent association with their humbler brethren they were taught to

113

understand the harder realities of life. The Crown Prince himself had been the first of his house to enter a public university. In the case of his two sons, a more striking departure from ancient usage was decided upon, and when Prince William was fifteen years of age, and Prince Henry twelve, they were sent to the Gymnasium at Cassel, which occupies the place in Germany of one of our greater public schools. They were left by their parents, who accompanied them thither, in charge of General Richard von Gottberg, their military governor, and Dr. Georg Hinzpeter, their former tutor. Prince William, who was placed at once in one of the higher forms, passed his final examinations after some two years' study, and when he came of age in 1877, on completing his 18th year, quitted Cassel to join the regiment in which his father had also begun his military career, nearly thirty years before. Prince Henry, who was destined for a naval career, on leaving Cassel, joined the cadet ship *Niobe*, at Kiel, and after a year's apprenticeship, started in the *Prince Adalbert* for a two year's cruise round the world. The two young Princes inherited from their mother their taste for English games and field sports. The first lawn-tennis court in Berlin and Potsdam, where the game is now growing popular, was, needless to say, in the gardens of the New Palace; the river Havel, with its wooded lakes, was near for bathing and boating; and on a little model frigate presented by our King William IV to King Frederick William III of Prussia, they learned their first essays in navigation. There is no one who follows with a keener interest all great events ill the world of sport and athletics in England than the present German Emperor William II.

The youngest daughter of the Crown Prince and Princess was born on the 22nd of April, 1872, and named Margaret, after her godmother **Margherita**, the reigning Queen of Italy, who came to Potsdam for the christening ceremonies. The close friendship of the heirs to the thrones of Germany and Italy was bearing fruit, for in the following year (1873) King Victor Emmanuel, who until the downfall of the French Empire had from a sense of obligation maintained sympathetic relations with the Emperor Napoleon, paid a visit to the Court of Berlin, which was returned by the Crown Prince immediately, and by the Emperor himself as soon as public duty admitted of his absenting himself from the capital. Latterly there were few years when business or pleasure did not take the Crown Prince over the Alps. Many will remember, with special interest at the present time, an incident which occurred during his visit to Rome in 1878, when he went as the Emperor's representative to attend the funeral of the founder of the new Italian kingdom. Appearing on the balcony of the Quirinal with King Humbert and Queen Margherita, he lifted the little Prince of Naples in his arms to show him to the people. The quick imagination of the Roman crowd seized on the symbolic side of this natural movement, and gave vent to the most enthusiastic demonstrations of delight.

In the same year, after the marriage of his eldest daughter, Princess Charlotte, with Bernhard, Hereditary Prince of Saxe-Meiningen, the Crown Prince had accompanied the Crown Princess to England. During their visit to Hatfield House in the beginning of June came the news of the desperate attempt of the socialist Karl Nobiling on the life of the Emperor William. The evening after the receipt of this alarming news the Crown Prince and Princess were once more in Berlin, where the Government was placed in the Prince's hands during the Emperor's

115

temporary disablement.

It was not until the last month of 1878 that the aged Monarch was sufficiently recovered to resume the reins of government. During these six months the Congress of Berlin had met and separated. One famous State document, bearing the Crown Prince's signature, belongs to this period of the Regency, a letter to Pope Leo XIII, at the moment when those negotiations with the Vatican were reopened, which paved the way for an ultimate reconciliation. The following extract contains the two essential points: the firm determination of the Prussian Sovereign to remain independent of the control of the Church, and the profession of readiness to approach the questions at issue in a conciliatory spirit: -

'The demand advanced in your letter of the 17th of April, that the constitution and the laws of Prussia should be modified to meet the principles of the Roman Catholic Church, is one which no Prussian Sovereign will be able to admit, because the independence of the monarchy, which it is now my duty to defend, as an inheritance received from my fathers and an obligation owed to my country, would cease to be absolute if the free development of its legislation were to be subordinated to the control of another power without. Though it is therefore not in my power, and perhaps not in that of your Holiness either, to remove an antagonism of principles, which has for a thousand years been more keenly felt in the history of Germany than in that of any other country, I am nevertheless prepared to meet the difficulties which both parties have inherited in this conflict, in the peace-loving and conciliatory spirit which my convictions as a Christian enjoin.'

When the brief period of Regency was over the Crown Prince resumed his quiet, unobtrusive life once more; but there was no work of public utility, no historic centenary, no inauguration of national monuments in which he did not take his part, sometimes by the side of the Emperor, sometimes as his representative. The Winter which followed these troublous times was indeed a sad one for the royal household - in December Princess Alice died, and in March fell the crushing blow which has been already alluded to, the death of the beloved Prince Waldemar.

The small English community of Berlin was sure of the Crown Prince's interest and protection, and the building of the English church, in the gardens of the Monbijou Palace, with the funds which were collected on the occasion of the Silver Wedding, was a source of continual occupation to the Crown Princess, who studied every detail herself with an artist's care. There is a pleasant memory of home about the little church, prettily situated in the Palace garden, and its completion was the realization of a long cherished dream. The speech made by the Crown Prince at the ceremony of laying the foundation stone will be especially interesting to English readers: -

'1 feel,' he said, 'a peculiar pleasure in addressing those who have met together to-day to witness the laying of the foundation-stone of the first English church in this town; for this act realizes a hope which not the Crown Princess alone, but I also, have long cherished. The fulfilment of this hope, however, seemed very difficult, and would have remained so, but for the efforts, not only of the English congregation, but also of many friends and well-wishers both in England and here. I dwell with pleasure on the thought that the Emperor, in granting the use of this piece of Crownland, has been actuated by the same feelings which prompted his brother and predecessor, King Frederick William IV, to appropriate one of the rooms of the Palace of Monbijou to the use of the English congregation, who had till then held their church services in a room at an hotel. I am glad that the anniversary of the Queen's birthday has been chosen for laying the foundation-stone of the English church, especially as the Queen's recent bereavement[2] prevents any other celebration of the day this year. The Prince of Wales and the other members of the Royal Family are certainly present with us in spirit to-day, for to their zealous efforts is chiefly owing the success of the fete in London which provided so large a portion of the funds for the building and carrying out of the plans, furnished by the talent of the eminent Berlin architect. Professor Raschdorff.

'The Crown Princess and I shall always take an additional interest in the church, because you know that the English residents, while providing it for their own worship, intend it at the same time to be a memorial of the 25th anniversary of our wedding day. Let me conclude by expressing every good wish for the perfect success of the undertaking, and the hope that it may contribute towards making their foreign home more home-like to the English residents in Berlin.'

'I am quite proud of my English,' said the Crown Prince, in giving the manuscript of this speech to Mr. Teignmouth Shore, who had been most active in promoting the scheme. 'I wrote it all out myself.'

In this connection also may be mentioned an incident recorded by Mr. Perry at an interview in

Buckingham Palace, many years after the old days at Bonn.

'After kind enquiries,' Mr. Perry writes, 'about my children, whose names he remembered after so many years, he took a little prayer-book from his desk, and holding it out to me, asked me if 1 remembered it. I did not. 'You lent me that,' he said, 'one Sunday when I came into your seat in the English church at Bonn, and 1 kept it, and always carry it about with me. 1 like your English service so much.'

And so the years went by brightly and usefully, in spite of the ever-increasing difficulty of the position, as the heir to the throne grew older, witnessing in due course the marriage of Prince William to Princess Augusta Victoria of Schleswig-Holstein, witnessing the birth of grandchildren, and all the lights and shadows of home-life, varied by continual journeys as duty called or pleasure; for the wandering spirit acquired in youth was strong to the last. One of these journeys calls for more than a passing record. It was towards the close of 1883 that the Crown Prince was charged to return on the King's behalf the visit that King Alfonso of Spain had paid to the Prussian capital. Circumstances had rendered it expedient that the nearer route through France should be abandoned, and the journey made by sea from Genoa to Valencia. The advent of the Prince in Italy was invariably marked by popular demonstrations of affection; and late as the hour was when the Royal party arrived in Genoa, the streets were thronged to receive him, for it was still fresh in the people's memory that the Crown Prince and Princess had initiated an appeal to their own countrymen on behalf of the sufferers in the recent calamity of Ischia.[3] After spending the night in the Royal Palace, he embarked on the *Prince Adalbert*, the vessel on which his son had sailed round the world, and arrived at Valencia, after a stormy passage, on the 22nd of November. At Madrid every form of festivity was instituted in his honour; and at the Court Ball the veteran General von Blumenthal, who accompanied him, was forced to take part in the royal quadrille, a performance which he said weighed more heavily on him than the prospect of another campaign would have done.

All was new ground to the Crown Prince, who spent every available moment in the picture galleries, and after a fortnight at Madrid he devoted another week to a tour among the classic cities, finding a new revelation of Art in the marvels of the Alhambra, in the great Mosque, with its thousand columns of the city of the Caliphs, in the vast design of the Cathedral of Seville. During his stay at Madrid a telegram reached him from Berlin, instructing him to return by Rome, ostensibly to thank the King for his hospitality at Genoa, but also to afford an opportunity for a visit to the Pope, whose conciliatory policy promised to effect an end so ardently desired by the Emperor William, the re-establishment of peace with the Catholic Church and party. In Home the Crown Prince was the guest of the King at the Quirinal. A visit direct from the Quirinal to the Vatican could scarcely, in the actual state of relations, have been acceptable. A curious compromise was therefore resorted to. From the Quirinal the Prince drove first to the German Embassy. Thence he proceeded to the official residence of the Prussian Minister accredited to the Pope, and there, dismounting from the carriage which bore the arms of the house of Savoy, he drove with his Staff in the carriages of the Prussian Legation to the Vatican. He had previously disarmed the possibility of misinterpretation on the part of the national party, by placing, in the morning, a wreath on the grave of King Victor Emmanuel. There was no other person present at his interview with the Pope, and what passed remained at the time subject for conjecture. The incident is introduced here not on account of its political aspect, but in illustration of the admirable tact and judgment through which the Prince succeeded in offending neither party. 'Being the guest of the King of Italy,' he said himself, 'I have also been able to pay a visit to the Pope. These are facts of great importance, of which our country will reap the benefit.'

The mention of Rome recalls the memory of one who, having witnessed there the solution of the Italian question, was during thirteen years the Queen's representative at Berlin, and who acquired, as few foreigners could ever hope to do, the confidence both of the Court and the Government. In Lord Ampthill, gifted as he was in an extraordinary measure with social and intellectual charm, the Crown Prince and Princess found a warm friend, and they took the greatest pleasure in the society both of himself and of his wife - a friend of the Crown Princess's early days. His little villa on the hill near Sans Souci was a favourite spot with them, and the scene of many cherished recollections. An admirable scholar and a qualified critic, he was at the same time a thorough man of the world, a master of the literature of four languages, and he possessed the gift of expression in each; his mind was a storehouse of memories and portraits, and while it was a privilege to listen to his conversation, he possessed the rare and lovable quality of seeming to bestow his best upon whomsoever he might for the moment be in contact with. His early death, in 1884, was a great grief and a genuine loss to the royal pair, in whose lives he had become such a familiar figure. The day after his death the Crown Prince came himself to the little villa to lay a wreath upon the coffin, and he took a rosebud from it away with him to keep.

When in the summer of 1886 the University of Heidelberg: celebrated its fifth centenary the Crown Prince was again the Emperor's representative. His speech on this occasion, apart from its intrinsic merit, and its telling force in the mouth of one who was looked on as the typical representative of United Germany, has also a touching interest from the fact that it is the last important public speech which he ever made in that clear, familiar, ringing voice of his. So soon after the shadows began to close around him, and the silence fell. This speech, which inevitably loses much in translation, is so remarkable that it shall be given unabridged. Addressing himself to the Grand Duke of Baden as Chancellor, and the assembled University, he said: -

'As bearer of the greetings and congratulations of His Majesty the Emperor, I am filled with pride and pleasure at the enthusiasm with which on these festal days her sons, both young and old, have gathered round their princely Chancellor, looking back with him on the glorious history of this University, and realizing, with gratitude to God, that in the 500 years of her existence she has never known a brighter period than that in which we live. Founded in the dawn of our age of culture, the University of Heidelberg has experienced and shared in all the changeful phases through which the German character has passed, in the hard-won development of its individuality. She has flourished and drooped in turn; suffered and battled for the freedom of belief and research; has known sorrow and exile, that at last, supported by the firm and gentle hand of her royal protector, she might cover her honourable wounds with the gala robe of victory.

'Like the German nation, whose noblest possessions her voice was ever raised to defend, she has seen fulfilled the desire of centuries. Her shield of honour gleams the brighter in the sun of our united Fatherland. With deep emotion I recall to-day the momentous hour[4] in which your Royal Highness was the first to greet the leader of our victorious nation by the noble name of Emperor. This recollection has for me a deep significance at the festival which we are celebrating. To be the first to put in action a great and good resolve is a privilege of your illustrious house and of this famous University.

'It is my pleasant duty in the mission I fulfil to acknowledge to her honour how loyally Heidelberg performed her part in fostering those mental and social conditions which were the first step to our national regeneration. She was ever liberally hospitable to teachers as to pupils. From every province they flocked to her, and in the loving arms of their Alma Mater, they realized once more that a greater mother was their parent.

'So here in the quiet of the student's life was developing what history, after long wanderings, has vouchsafed us. In the south-western corner of the Empire, near the old frontier, and therefore near the danger, the son of the North learned to love the son of the South as his brother, that he might return again to his home, and spread abroad the fair faith that all the people are one people, which faith is our treasure and our strength.

'And now that we possess it once more, this blessing of unity, there is blown back from the mighty whole a breath which brings vigour to the dear old home where we were educated. Wider grow the aims of knowledge, wider our aspirations, more grateful the duty of the teacher to proclaim them, and of the pupil to appreciate them.

'The Fatherland and the Academic Commonwealth can only exercise a beneficial influence on one another if they preserve the same virtues in their respective spheres of activity. The higher the results we achieve in science and in history, the loftier the aims to which we aspire, the greater prudence and self-denial we shall need.

'My dearest wishes and my confident hope, which I offer to the University to-day, are recorded in the appeal I make to teachers and to scholars, to bear in mind the duty most imperiously devolving on us, when elated with success, in learning as in living, to be conscientious and severe in intellectual discipline, and to promote the feeling of brotherhood among comrades, that from the spirit of independence and the love of peace may ensue the necessary force to develop all the forms of our national life. So may it be granted to this University, one of the oldest schools of German culture, to remain in energy her youngest.'

In the Winter a severe cold brought on a hoarseness, which was not at first regarded as of serious importance, and was lightly treated by the Emperor himself, who would say with a smile, "I cannot sing,' apologizing for his enforced silence. But as the weeks went by, and no improvement was revealed, there were not a few who began to feel a certain anxiety; and the festivities on the 22nd of

March, when the Emperor William attained his ninetieth birthday, and Prince Henry was formally betrothed to his cousin, Princess Irene of Hesse, when he was called upon to represent the aged Monarch at a number of functions, were a severe strain upon his overtaxed energies, A cure at Ems was recommended, but proved of no service; and it was after his return from Ems that those sinister rumours first began to spread abroad, which enlisted for the royal patient not only the sympathy of Germany, but that of Europe and of countries far beyond the seas, where his name had become a proverb for all that was lovable and generous and of good report; a sympathy which, we have the Chancellor's guarantee for it, was the one source of gratification and consolation to the last dark weeks of the aged Emperor's waning life.

He was nevertheless well enough to take part in the rejoicings at Queen Victoria's Jubilee, and as he rode in the procession in the white uniform of the Cuirassiers his stately presence and his kindly, friendly face, together with the sentiment of some grave crisis hanging over the head of the soldier-hero, made a deep and lasting impression on all who were present at that memorable scene. Men spoke of nothing but the German Crown Prince, as if they, too, had a special claim upon him. They knew that he was gifted with all the virtues which Englishmen admire, and that he loved our country well, and through the dark year that followed there was but one topic that all were absorbed in, one prayer that went up through the length and breadth of the land, that this man's life might be spared. It will have a pathetic interest to many who were witnesses of the last great public ceremony in which he took part to know what was passing in his own mind as he rode past, the observed of all observers. His quick observation was at work, noting upon that day, as he ever did in foreign countries, anything which struck him as worthy of admiration, with a view to its subsequent adaptation in his own. After his death was found in a little pocket-book, which he carried with him on that day, the following entry: 'The ambulance arrangements on the day of the Jubilee. The drinking-troughs for horses and dogs, and the cabmen's shelters in the streets of London.'

From London the Crown Prince went alone for a brief visit to Scotland, and appeared to derive great benefit from the fresh mountain air and the vigorous life he led. During his stay at Braemar he was asked by a gentleman to do him the honour of christening a steam-launch. He gave it the name of 'The White Heather', showing how his thoughts still travelled back to the memory of a day, nearly thirty years before, when in these same Scotch mountains he had plucked the sprig of white heather to give to his English bride. Rejoining the Crown Princess and his three youngest daughters, the Crown Prince went from Scotland to Toblach, in Tyrol, and later to Venice and Baveno. Finally, the Villa Zirio, at San Remo, was chosen as a Winter residence, and when he re-entered Berlin it was as German Emperor. The events of last year are still too fresh in the memory of all to need recapitulation here. We all remember too well the changing hopes and fears, the doubts that trembled into certainty, and left no room for hope. It was a gloomy New Year at Berlin; and when the usual season of Carnival came round there as but little heart in the gaiety. Ever thoughtful of others, and mindful how important an interest is involved in the social season to large numbers of the working-classes, the Crown Prince had sent a message from San Remo, desiring that all should take its usual course; but at

every meeting there was present an unbidden guest -
the sinister rumour passing through the throng.
February the 9th, the day upon which the operation
of tracheotomy was performed, had been fixed for the
annual subscription ball in the Royal Opera House,
the proceeds of which are devoted to the Berlin
charities. The house was full, as ever, but through the
dense crowd the unwelcome news began to spread,
and there was no mirth in any of the thousand faces -
not a dance was danced that night, and all the people
seemed touched as by the sense of a personal sorrow.
A month later anxious crowds were gathered round
the Palace in Berlin. The Emperor was sinking from
the exhaustion of age; far from the son who had been
ever at his side in the hour of danger, he fought the
last great battle alone. But gently sleep fell upon him,
full of years and full of honour, and without a struggle,
the long laborious life was closed.

Frederick William, German Crown Prince

VII.

1888.

O N the night of the 11th of March the
Emperor Frederick reached his
capital, in a wild storm of sleet and
snow; he had borne the journey well,
and the few who witnessed his arrival were struck by
his vigorous demeanour. His old friend and ally, King
Humbert, had travelled to Genoa to salute him as
Emperor on his way, and the last meeting between the
two Sovereigns, whose lives had had so much in
common, was a very touching one. All along the line
from the German frontier, thousands had flocked to
every railway station in the hope of obtaining a
fleeting glimpse of the illustrious traveller, and silently
but sincerely his people welcomed him home. The
Chancellor and the Ministers of State had gone as far
as Leipzig to meet the Royal train, and transact with
the Emperor such immediate business as required his
personal direction. On his arrival, shortly after eleven,
the Emperor drove straight to the Palace of
Charlottenburg, which gives its name to a suburb
some three miles from the city. A little later, through
the white snow-covered Linden Alley, lined by troops
with flaming torches, the body of Emperor William,
dressed in his military cap and cloak, with the Order
of 'Merit' on his breast, was solemnly borne from the

Palace to the Cathedral where he was to lie in State.

On the following day the Emperor Frederick issued his proclamation to the German nation, and a rescript addressed to the Imperial Chancellor was simultaneously published, in which he paid a warm tribute of esteem to his father's faithful friend and counsellor, and set forth the principles which were to characterize his government. These two remarkable documents, which will be found in the Appendix, composed entirely by the Emperor's own hand, would alone suffice to mark his brief and tragic reign, and their lessons will not all be lost. At last, after the long years of waiting and restraint, his own heart might find expression; and now, when the power came, it was already too late. He was not even able to look for the last time on the father he had loved and served so well; only from the window of his palace he watched the funeral procession winding past to the Mausoleum in the garden of Charlottenburg, where Queen Louise and King Frederick William III lie side by side in their marble sleep. It was a moving scene to many a war-worn veteran, that last farewell to the good old Emperor; it was a moving scene to all who had lived through the mighty changes that his reign had witnessed; but what must have been in the mind of the illustrious mourner, as he turned back from the window into his silent chamber! He also had meant to be his people's father; he had prepared himself with untiring devotion to duty for his great task, the thought of which in times before had almost overwhelmed him till his strong faith reconquered his misgivings of himself: he had not neglected to make acquaintance with people of every party, class, and calling, so as to be in touch with the inner life and aspirations of the nation; he had kept his life clean and spotless, and above all littleness and spite, to be a bright example in the eyes of men. And now, when he came to be crowned at last, there was nothing left him to do but to husband what strength remained to him for the daily routine of duties that he must needs fulfil, to give up all the rest for ever, bravely to surrender himself and bow to the will of God. The service of man had been his lifelong study, and now, when the time for realization should have come, it was only given him to teach one lesson, but that the hardest of all to learn and the noblest of all to teach, the lesson of self-renouncement and unmurmuring resignation. To the last his force of will maintained him, worn and harassed as he was by all that his disease entailed upon him, and by the oppression of his enforced silence, he left no portion of his daily task undone, and on the sick-bed where others rest he still worked bravely on. When he was well enough to spend the afternoons in the garden of the Palace, he would send for his horses, and watch his favourites being exercised with a look of wistful interest. His love for animals was great; from his earliest youth he had made a certain race of Italian greyhounds his particular pets, and was always to he seen in the country followed by two or three of these delicate and graceful animals, and not a day had passed in old times, either in Berlin or Potsdam, without his visiting the stables to feed with his own hand the horses who knew his footsteps and expected his daily visit.

Day after day through the Spring weeks dense crowds hung round the Charlottenburg Palace, in spite of its great distance from Berlin, for the chance of seeing that beloved face at the window, or of catching a passing glimpse of him when later, as the weather mended, a few short drives were sanctioned. If the love and care of all who surrounded him, if the sympathy and admiration of the world were any consolation to the strong mind for its forced inactivity, to the strong man for his waning strength, such consolation was not wanting; and indeed it was a theme to which he constantly recurred, the sincere feeling evinced for him in foreign countries, and what most particularly touched him, the expression this feeling found in France. This is no place to intrude upon the ministries of that closer circle that watched his sick chamber and tended his latter days with loving and unwearying devotion, but probably never has it been granted to any single individual to find such a place as he found, by the mute appeal of his pathetic story, in the hearts of all classes and all countries.

There were three bright passages in the brief three months of his reign, with the daily record of which all are still familiar. The first was Queen Victoria's visit to Berlin, during which he perceptibly rallied; the second, the marriage of his sailor son, Prince Henry, to Princess Irene of Hesse, at which he was able to be present; and the third, the move from Charlottenburg to the old home at Potsdam, to which he now gave the name of 'Friedrichskron'; the palace where he was born, where he had spent the happy Summers of his married days, and where he was now all too soon to close his bright and useful life. The last crisis set in very soon after his arrival at Friedrichskron, and his state was declared to be hopeless. Brave and patient as lie had been throughout his long and cruel illness, with its wearing and painful recurrent crises, bravely as he had received his death-warrant, so bravely he met his end.

The 14th of June was the birthday of Princess Sophie. He sent for her quite early in the morning to give her the flowers he had ordered for her, and seemed quite cheerful and bright, but his strength was exhausted by the progress of the disease and his long heroic struggle against it. To the end he had 'done out the duty,' he had suffered without complaining, as through life he had kept his great shield white, and now the silent Emperor bowed his head, and was ready, if ever man was on earth, to meet God face to face. A little before midday on the 15th of June, surrounded by the whole of his family, he passed away without a struggle.

After death, his body was by his own express wish wrapped in his military mantle, and the Empress placed in his arms the sword he had worn in his various campaigns; round his neck she hung his Grand Cross of the Order 'Pour le Mérite,' and on his breast she laid the wreath of oak leaves she had given him on his return from the war of 1870.

His coffin was placed in the church where his sons Prince Sigismund and Prince Waldemar rest, in the gardens of Sans Souci, awaiting the Mausoleum that is to be built to receive it. The funeral ceremony took place upon the day of Waterloo, a bright day between rainy days, and never were the parks and gardens of Friedrichskron more beautiful than on that morning, with the fresh green of the late season, and the birds singing in all the trees.

In the great semi-circular garden in front of the Palace, facing the avenue which leads to Sans Souci, the solemn procession formed; under the trees surrounding it troops were drawn up, to the left infantry, to the right cavalry, amongst which were the Life Guards with black cuirasses: there was no crowding, the public were excluded here; along the avenue more troops were drawn up waiting to join the procession. The coffin lay in the Jasper Hall, opening on a terrace facing the garden, and there a preliminary service took place. Then as the coffin was placed upon the bier, the soft and solemn singing ceased, and the military bands stationed round the semi-circle began a weird and melancholy music, chorales of the German Protestant Church, each taking up the other, and so on down the avenue till the sound died away in the trees. All the while muffled drums were beating. The procession formed; the charger he had ridden in the war of 1870, a superb chestnut, called Wörth, which knew him and followed him as a dog does its master, was led behind the bier, and the veteran Field-Marshal von Blumenthal carried the Imperial banner. It was a small procession, but very solemn and impressive. The sun shone out on the helmets and cuirasses, on the gardens he had loved and cared for, on the terrace where he walked in the Summer evenings in pleasant converse with some favoured guest, while amid the weird music of the military bands, and the roll of the muffled drums, the slow procession was lost in the green of the trees.

And now in conclusion let us glance back over the career and character of this singularly gifted life. The time allotted him to reign in was too brief and troubled for the accomplishment of any public acts that could leave a permanent trace behind them; but the whole tendency of his example, the note of idealism which he supplied to temper the sterner material virtues of the national character, his breadth and tolerance in questions of religion, the consistent record of his simple and unselfish life, will not be soon effaced, and will some day be better understood. The genius of each nation is different, and we should do ill to judge the German by our own, or to expect that like causes would necessarily lead to like effects, but the genius of every vigorous nation is progressive, and it was his merit as a ruler to have appreciated this.

To those who never knew him, it will be impossible to convey an adequate idea of his irresistible personal charm, of the smile in his eyes, and the kindly brightness of his face, which brought a contagious light and gladness wherever he entered in. His sense of humour was keen, and like all simple characters in whom the child is only gone to sleep, he delighted in innocent amusement. While none the less, though known only to his closest intimates, there lay beneath this outward brightness the inevitable accompaniment of the idealistic nature, the 'eternal note of sadness', the deep depression of the earnest thinker. All who were brought into contact with him fell immediately under the charm of his manner, which, with all its naturalness and geniality, was never wanting in dignity. And where such acquaintance ripened into closer intimacy, experience only developed a warmer admiration. To quote once again the words of one who had exceptional opportunities for studying his character in the most trying times, in camp and on the battlefield: 'He was not only the most lovable, but the noblest man with whom I have ever associated - noble in his acts, noble in his speech, noble in his judgment of others. I never knew him say an unkind thing of anyone, man or woman, living or dead - not that his judgment of others was always favourable, but it was never expressed in other than the most kindly terms.'[1]

Destined from his birth to rule, he schooled himself to learn submission, and to abide his time in patience. Free to command the energies of his subordinates, he was full of kindly consideration, and never suffered custom to blunt his gratitude for a service loyally performed. Though constantly engaged in the public duties of his lofty station, he still found time for all those private acts of kindliness and sympathy, as neighbour, as master, as friend, which earn for private persons the love and admiration of their fellows. He had acquired wide and varied learning, and his high ambition was to open a royal road to knowledge to the richest and the poorest of his subjects alike. For him the earth displayed her marvels to a loving eye, and Art not vainly revealed her treasures; he had seen much, toiled much, enjoyed much. He was essentially a man, and there was no human interest or emotion which he could not share.

An active and industrious youth, a married life crowned with many blessings, and not untempered by the sorrows man is heir to, and a public career which was rich in great results, had prepared him for a brilliant and useful future. All too early, too soon for the accomplishment of many cherished plans, after an heroic endurance of pain and disappointment, he was taken from us in the pride of his manlihood and strength; and as they bore him on that Summer morning from his happy home of thirty years, there came into the present writer's mind the words: -

> "Thou art the ruins of the noblest man
> That ever lived in the tide of times."

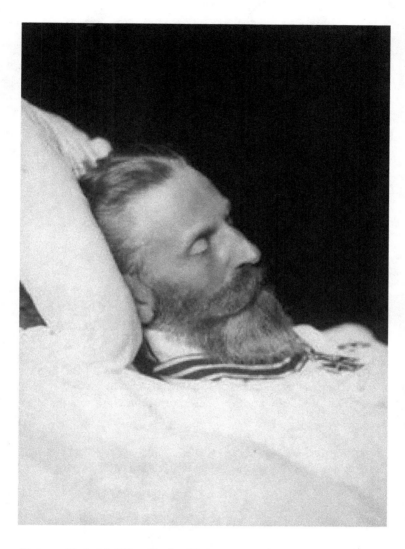

Emperor Frederick III on his deathbed

FOOTNOTES

I.

1. Rudolf V. Zastrow and Count Adolf Konigsmark.
2. This letter is given in full in *L'Empereur Frédéric* by Edouard Simon (1888), from which this extract is translated.

III.

1. The Prince Consort died on December the 14th, 1861.
2. Sir Charles Lock Eastlake (1793-1865), President of the Royal Academy and first Director of the National Gallery.
3. *The Times*, May 5, 1862.
4. Immanuel Kant (1724-1804), regarded as the leading figure in European philosophy of his age.

IV.

1. Meningitis cerebralis.

V.

1. Spicheren and Saarbrück.
2. A full account of this institution has been published by Miss Florence Lees (Mrs. Craven), a renowned nurse who was one of the ablest of Florence Nightingale's pupils and worked extensively with her.

VI.

1. In an eloquent and touching speech, at a meeting held on the 1st of July, 1888, Dr. Richard Schone, the Director-General of the Royal Berlin Museums, summed up the great services rendered to Art by the departed Emperor. He enumerated the new Museums that had been inaugurated under his fostering hand, and described the efforts made by him to place the collections at Berlin on a footing of equality with those of other countries. The excavations at Olympia, he added, would remain a permanent monument of his zeal for, and devotion to, knowledge. 'In the midst of a whole nation's mourning,' he said, 'they may scarcely venture to raise their voices, whose privilege it was to serve and to labour under him, in that more restricted field to which the Emperor Frederick, as Crown Prince, on behalf of his Imperial father, bestowed his special protection. But if, as long as the light of his eyes was not darkened, our mouths were closed in respectful reserve, now, at least, that he has gone from us, we may be permitted, over his grave, to give full expression to the reverence, the love, and the unalterable gratitude, which we had learned to feel for him.'
2. The death of Leopold, Duke of Albany (1853-84), youngest son of Queen Victoria and thus brother-in-

law of Crown Prince Frederick William.

3. A volcanic island at the northern end of the Gulf of Naples, which was struck by an earthquake in July 1883 with the loss of an estimated 4,000 lives.

4. At the ceremony at Versailles, when the Emperor assumed the Imperial dignity, the Grand Duke of Baden was the first to step forward and call for a cheer for the 'German Emperor.'

VII.

1. General Sir Beauchamp Walker. Letter to the Author.

APPENDIX.

THE EMPEROR FREDERICK'S PROCLAMATION TO HIS PEOPLE.

The Emperor's glorious life is ended.

In the dearly-loved father whom I mourn, and for whom all the members of my Royal House are with me sorrowing, Prussia's loyal people has lost a King crowned with glory, the German nation has lost the founder of its unity, the re-established Empire has lost the first German Emperor.

His exalted name will remain indissolubly connected with all the greatness of the German Fatherland, in re-creating which the persistent labour of Prussia's people and Princes has found its fairest reward.

In raising the Prussian Army with unwearying and paternal care to the height of its grave mission, King William established the sure foundation of those victories which were won under his leadership by German arms, and from which the national unity arose. He thus secured the Empire that powerful position for which till then every German heart had longed, but hardly dared to hope.

And what he won for his people in the fire and sacrifice of battle it was granted him to establish and promote, through long laborious years of government consecrated to the work of peace.

Resting secure on her own strength, Germany stands respected in the councils of the nations, and only desires to enjoy and develop what she had won, in peace.

That this is so, we must thank the Emperor William. His constant fidelity to duty, his unremitting energy, labouring only for the good of the Fatherland, supported as he was by the self-sacrificing devotion which the Prussian nation has ever unwaveringly shown, and all the German races have shared.

On me have now devolved all the rights and duties, bound up with the throne of my House, which I am resolved faithfully to observe so long as it may please God's will that 1 shall reign.

Deeply conscious of the greatness of my task, my sole endeavour will be to carry on the work in the sense in which it was beg-un, to make Germany a stronghold of peace, and in harmony with the federal governments, as well as with the constitutional bodies of the Empire and of Prussia, to further the prosperity of the country.

To my loyal people, which has through the story of many centuries stood by my House in good and evil days, I place my unreserved, confidence. For I am convinced that, resting on the basis of the inseparable union between Prince and people, which, independently of all changes in political life, has been the imperishable heritage of the House of

Hohenzollern, my throne will ever be as sure as the prosperity of the country which I am now called upon to govern, to which I promise and vow to be a just and faithful King, in joy as well as in sorrow.

May God grant me His blessing and strength for this work, to which henceforth I dedicate my life.

FREDERICK, I.R.

Berlin, March 12, 1888.

RESCRIPT ADDRESSED TO THE IMPERIAL CHANCELLOR.

My Dear Prince,

At the opening of my reign I feel the necessity of addressing you, for so many years the tried first servant of my father, now resting in God. You were the faithful and courageous counsellor who gave form to the aims of his policy, and secured their successful realization.

To you the warm thanks of myself and of my House are in duty due.

You have, therefore, a right, before all others, to know what are the guiding principles by which my rule will be governed.

The constitutional and legal ordinances of the Empire and of Prussia must first and foremost be consolidated in the respect of the nation and in the national life. Therefore, those shocks which repeated changes in the institutions and laws of the State entail are to be avoided as far as it is possible.

The furtherance of the duties which fall to the Imperial Government must leave those stable principles undisturbed upon which hitherto the

Prussian State has securely rested.

In the Empire the constitutional rights of all the Federal Governments are to be as conscientiously observed as those of the Imperial Diet; but from both a similar respect for the rights of the Emperor will be expected. At the same time it must be kept in view that these mutual rights are only intended to serve the promotion of the public welfare, which remains the supreme law, and that new and undoubted national requirements which may make themselves felt must be satisfied in full measure.

The most indispensable and most certain guarantee for the unimpeded furtherance of this work I hold to be the maintenance in unabated strength of the defensive forces of the nation, my well-tried army, and my growing navy, which is finding important duties to perform, now that we have acquired possessions beyond the seas. Both must continually maintain that standard of efficiency and thoroughness of organization which have already established their fame, and guarantee their effective service in the future.

I am resolved to govern in the Empire and in Prussia with a conscientious observation of the the provisions of their respective constitutions. For these were established by those who have gone before me in wise appreciation of the inevitable requirements of social and political life, and the questions it presents for solution, and must be respected by each and all, that their vigour and beneficent influence may be assured.

It is my will that the principle of religious toleration, which has for years been held sacred in my family, shall continue to extend its protection to all my subjects, to whatsoever religious community and creed they may belong. Every one of them stands equally near my heart, for all of them equally in the hour of danger proved their complete devotion.

In entire accord with the views of my imperial father, I shall warmly support every movement towards furthering the economical prosperity of every class of society, reconciling their conflicting interests, and mitigating, as far as may be possible, unavoidable differences, without encouraging the anticipation that every social evil can be removed by State intervention.

I consider as intimately connected with social questions the control of the education of youth. While, on the one hand, a higher cultivation must be extended to ever-widening circles, we have at the same time to beware of the dangers of half-education, of awakening demands which the nation's economic development is unable to satisfy, of neglecting the real business of education in a one-sided effort after increase of knowledge.

Only a generation growing up on the sound principle of the fear of God, and in simplicity of morals, will possess sufficient power of resistance to counteract the dangers which the whole community incurs in a time of rapid economic development, through the example of the highly luxurious life of individuals. It is my will that no opportunity be lost in the public service of manifesting all possible opposition to the temptation to inordinate expenditure.

My unbiassed consideration is assured in advance

146

to every proposal of financial reform, if the old Prussian principle of economy will not enable us to avoid the imposition of new burdens, and to effect an alleviation of the demands that have hitherto been made.

I consider as beneficial the measure of self-government accorded to greater and smaller communities in the State. On the other hand, I suggest for examination the point whether the right of levying taxes conferred upon these communities, which is exercised by them without sufficient regard to the burdens simultaneously imposed by the Empire and the State, may not press too heavily upon the individual.

In like manner it will have to be considered whether a reform in the direction of simplification may not be admissible in the organization of the authorities, so that by reducing the number of officials an increase might be made to their emoluments.

If we succeed in maintaining in full vigour the bases of political and social life, it will afford me especial satisfaction to assist in promoting to its perfect development the progress which Art and Science in Germany can boast in so large a measure.

For the realization of these my intentions, I count upon the devotion you have given such constant proof of, and the support of your tried experience.

May it be granted me on these principles to lead the people of Germany and Prussia to new honours in the field of practical development, with the unanimous co-operation of all the organs of the Empire, the devotion of the people's representatives,

147

and all the official bodies, with the responsive confidence of every class of the population in Germany and Prussia.

Not dazzled by the splendour of great achievements, I shall be content, if hereafter it be said of my government, that it was beneficial to my people, useful to my country, and a blessing to the Empire!

Your affectionate,

FREDERICK, I.R.

Berlin, March 12, 1888.

9 798648 856295